I0004324

Windows for

Beginners

By Walter Bragg

Copyright 2004 Walter Bragg
Beckley, West Virginia

Bragg_walter@hotmail.com
http://shotguns.vstorecomputers.com

This book is dedicated to my best friend Bear Dog.

Bear Dog passed away 11/26/04. He was a 14 years blond Akita and my best friend. Who death left a big empty whole in my heart and life. Bear Dog you are truly missed and can never be replaced.

Table of Contents

5

Disclaimer of Liability

Whilst every effort has been made to ensure and supply reliable, accurate, and up-to-date information, facts, and references to other materials and resources, it should be noted and understood that. As there are discrepancies between some of that information, materials and resources available. The Author gives NO guarantee as to the accuracy and conclusiveness of the said content. And no responsibility is accepted whatsoever for any resultant errors contained herein, or for any impairment. The information contained here has been researched, compiled, and based on independent data The views and opinions of authors expressed in this book does not warrant guarantee or assume any legal liability or responsibility for the accuracy, completeness, or usefulness of any information, product, or process disclosed. This book does not make any warranty, guarantees

Chapter 1

Learn Photoshop-- any version of Photoshop

Create multiple photo layouts in Photoshop Elements

When you take a picture, you want to be able to fit it in your wallet and 4x6, 5x7, and 8x10 picture frames. Instead of resizing the photo and pasting each size on a sheet of paper to print, have Elements automatically generate the sheet for you. Here is how:

1. Open the photo you want to appear in multiple sizes on one sheet of paper.
2. Click File, click Automate, and choose Picture Package.
3. When the Picture Package dialog box opens, check "Use front most document" under Source Image.
4. In the Document section, choose the combination of photo sizes you would like from the Layout pop-up menu (e.g. one 5x7 and eight wallet-size photos).
5. You can also choose the resolution of your image and the color mode. If your image is from a digital camera, leave the mode at RGB color. As a rule of thumb, you should not increase the resolution. If you do, you will soften the image and make it look a bit pixilated.
6. Click OK, sit back, and watch Photoshop Elements automatically make duplicates, resize the images, and place them onto one 8x10 sheet, ready to print.

Remove wrinkles like magic with Adobe Photoshop

People spend thousands of dollars on products to hide and reduce the appearance of wrinkles. But you can do your friends a favor and remove those wrinkles, crow's feet, and other signs of aging digitally. Here is how:

1. Open your photo.
2. Switch to the Healing Brush (its icon looks like a Band-Aid).
3. Hold the Option key on a Macintosh or the Alt key on a PC and click an area of smooth skin near the area you want to repair.
4. Drag the healing brush over the wrinkled area. Photoshop will remove the wrinkle while maintaining both the texture and detail of the skin.

You can use those same keyboard shortcuts to switch modes when using a paint or edit tool. For example, pressing Shift+Alt+M (or Shift-Option-M) when the paintbrush is active, paints in the Multiply mode. Press Shift+Alt+S (or Shift-Option-S) with the rubber stamp to clone in the Screen mode.

Also with brush modes, Photoshop gives you a few extra keys. The Q key selects the Behind mode, which paints behind the active layer. When painting in a black-and-white or indexed image, use the L key to switch to the Threshold mode and I for Dissolve.

When painting with the dodge or burn tool, the W, V, and Z keys switch between Shadows, Midtones, and Highlights. When using the sponge tool, J is for Desaturate and A is for Saturate. The only unused keys are P and R.

Working With Floating Selections

 Continuing the trend began in Version 4, Photoshop 5 makes floating selections more difficult to work with. Floaters no longer show up in the Layers palette, and you cannot set them down by pressing Command-E (Ctrl+E under Windows). The idea is to get you in the habit of using layers, which according to Adobe help

ensure the program is more stable. However, there are times--
particularly when working with masks-- when layers are not
available and floaters are your only option. Thankfully, not all is
lost. To mix the contents of a floater with the image below, choose
the Fade command under the Filter menu or press Command-Shift-
F (Ctrl+Shift+F under Windows). This command applies to filters,
color-adjustment commands, and now, floating selections.

Customizing the Full Screen Modes

As you undoubtedly know by now, you can cycle through
Photoshop's screen modes by pressing the F key. Pressing F once
hides the standard window elements-- scroll bars, title bar, status
bar-- and shows the image against a gray background. Press F
again to hide the menu bar and make the background black. Press
F a third time to restore the image window with scroll bars, menu
bar, and the rest.

Nevertheless, two little-known techniques involve the Shift key.
To change the gray area outside the image to some other color,
Shift-click in the gray area with the paint bucket tool. The next tip
works only in Photoshop 5: Press Shift-F to hide and display the
menu bar, regardless of the screen mode you are working in. This
means any time the menu bar disappears in Photoshop 5, you can
bring it back by pressing Shift-F. You never have to leave the full
screen mode again.

Mixing the Perfect Grayscale Image

Photoshop offers many ways to convert a full-color image to
grayscale. You can choose the Grayscale command and let the
program do all the work for you. You can select a single color
channel and choose Grayscale to dispose of the others. On the
other hand, you can convert to the Lab mode, switch to the
Lightness channel, and choose Grayscale to keep the device-
independent brightness values.

Photoshop 5 goes one better by permitting you to mix color channels manually. Choose the Channel Mixer from the Image: Adjust submenu. Then select the Monochrome check box to lose the colors. From then on, it is just a matter of editing the percentage values for each channel to come up with a mix that you like. To maintain a consistent level of brightness, make sure the sum of the percentages remains 100 percent. One might argue that you could already mix channels using the Calculations command, but Channel Mixer is significantly easier to use. Channel Mixer also permits you to mix all color channels at once, where Calculations is limited to two.

One thing: Channel Mixer does not convert the color mode. So after you apply the command, remember to choose Grayscale to dispose of the redundant channels.

Undoing Your Actions in the History Palette

The History palette is easily Photoshop 5's most liberating feature and the best implementation of multiple undos that I have ever seen. The palette lists up to 99 previous operations per each and every open image. This means you can apply 10 operations in Image A, switch to Image B and apply several thousand operations, and then return to Image A and undo any one of the first 10.

One of my favorite aspects Photoshop's implementation of multiple undos is that Ctrl+Z (Command-Z) remains the single-operation Undo/Redo toggle it has always been. To step back more than one operation, press Ctrl+Alt+Z (Command-Option-Z). To step forward, press Ctrl+Shift+Z (Command-Shift-Z). While this distinction might sound odd, it provides two benefits. First, it ensures that you do not backtrack accidentally. Ctrl+Z lets you bob up and down along the surface of the time line, the new shortcuts take you deeper.

Second, by keeping Undo and History separate, Photoshop makes it possible to undo actions performed in the History palette. Why do that? To compare before-and-after views of the image. First revert to a previous state by clicking on its name in the History palette. This is your "before" view. Now press Ctrl+Z to undo the state change and take you back to the most recent operation, which is the "after" view. Keep pressing Ctrl+Z to go back and forth, back and forth. Not only is this technique incredibly helpful for judging whether you are on the right track, its lightning fast as well.

Finally, the states in the History palette are not affected by saving or printing. To revert to an operation that you performed before saving, just press Ctrl+Alt+Z.

Magic Eraser Cum History Brush

Every state in the History palette serves as a separate snapshot. In addition, as with any snapshot in Photoshop, you can revert the entire image back to the snapped state, or restore selective areas using a brush. To do the latter, click in front of the state in the History palette from which you want to paint. This sets a paintbrush icon in the left-hand column, which identifies the state as the brush source. Now drag in the image window with the new history brush, which you can select from the keyboard by pressing the Y key. The history brush paints with the source state.

Note that this is also how the magic eraser works in Photoshop 5. When you Option-drag (or Alt+drag under Windows) with the eraser tool, Photoshop paints from the source state in the History palette, not from the saved image as in Photoshop 4.

Reverting a Selection

Photoshop 5 also lets you revert a selected area to a state in the History palette. First, click in front of the state that will serve as the source (as when preparing to use the history brush). Then press

Shift-Delete (or Shift+Backspace under Windows) to display the Fill dialog box and select the History option from the Use pop-up menu.

Want to bypass the Fill dialog box? After setting the source state, just press Command-Option-Delete (or Ctrl+Alt+Backspace) and Photoshop reverts the area immediately. One caveat: the source state must contain a corresponding layer for this technique to work.

Cloning Entire Layers

In Photoshop 4, you can clone selected areas by Command-Option-dragging (or Ctrl+Alt+dragging under Windows). However, you have to select an area for the technique to work. In Photoshop 5, you can now clone an entire layer by Command-Option-dragging, whether the layer is selected or not. To clone a whole layer when a selection is present, be sure to begin your drag outside the selection.

Pinpointing Points in the Curves Dialog Box

In Photoshop 4, the Levels and Curves commands are the primary means for adjusting brightness and contrast levels in an image. Curves are the more powerful tool, but Levels offers the advantages of a histogram and numerical options. In Photoshop 5, Curves still lacks a histogram, but you can enter specific brightness and ink-coverage values and edit them by the numbers.

But that's not all. Curves also help you identify specific points on a graph. To map a color from the image as a point on the graph. Ctrl+click (or Command-click on the Mac) on a pixel in the image window. Photoshop adds the point to the specific channel displayed in the dialog box. So if the RGB composite channel is visible, the point is added to the RGB composite curve. If the Red channel is visible, the point is added the point to the red graph, and so on. To add a color to each graph except the composite,

Ctrl+Shift+click (Command-Shift-click) on a pixel in the image window.

Naturally, when editing multiple graph points from the keyboard, it is helpful to be able to activate the points from the keyboard as well. To advance from one point on the graph to the next, press Ctrl+Tab (Command-Tab). To select the previous point, press Ctrl+Shift+Tab (Command-Shift-Tab). To deselect all points, press Ctrl+D (Command-D).

Keyboard Calculations

You probably take for granted that Photoshop lets you change the opacity of a layer by pressing a number key. Press the 5 key and the layer mixes 50/50 with the layers behind it, press 0 and it returns to full opacity. In Photoshop 5, you can do the same with blend modes (a k a calculations). First, select a selection or navigation tool. Then press Shift and Option plus a letter key on the Mac, or Shift and Alt under Windows. The letters you will want to memorize are N for Normal, M for Multiply, S for Screen, C for Color, and Y for Luminosity. There is also O for Overlay, F for Soft Light and H for Hard Light. D and B get you Color Dodge and Color Burn, respectively. The more obscure entries are K and G for Darken and Lighten; E and X for Difference and Exclusion, and U and T for Hue and Saturation.

Adobe Photoshop Elements

Photoshop Elements comes without professional tools such as CMYK separation and channel editing but retains a majority of Photoshop functionality -- and adds new interface makeovers. The software displays the familiar palette system. This system lets menu groups -- or palettes -- float over the workspace, giving users access to menu items without having to pull down the menus from the standard toolbar. Photoshop Elements includes several enhancements that should make it easy for beginners to use, but its function set is broad enough to satisfy the customization cravings of advanced users.

New palettes and browsers

Most noticeable on the interface is the Help Palette. When you place your mouse over an object in the tool palette or over one of the tools tabs, the Help Palette's contents change to show what that object or tab contains or does. For example, if you place your mouse over the sponge object, the Help Palette tells you that it can change the color saturation of an area. Furthermore, the palette contains a button that offers contextual help. With the sponge object, for example, pressing the help button will open the help info for the sponge tool.

We would have preferred that the Help Palette contain more information before we even click on the help button. Though slightly descriptive, the palette does not reveal enough about individual tools to be an aid to the beginner and is a waste of time for intermediate users.

More Cool Tools

Another convenient tool is the Filters Browser. Whenever you press this tab, a window opens to reveal thumbnails of filters that you can apply to your picture. Adobe uses a striped sailboat picture for its thumbnail, which helps to show what will happen to the picture before you apply the filter. To apply the desired filter, you either double-click on the thumbnail or drag it to your workspace. The Effects Browser works the same way, condensing to one-click effects that would normally take several steps to achieve, such as Blizzard or Drop Shadow.

We found the Filters and Effects browsers the most helpful in this new package. The Effects Browser, in particular, is a useful and easy-to-use time saving function.

With the addition of a Recipes Palette, Adobe attempts to reduce the number of clicks it takes to perform common image-editing tasks that usually take several steps. For example, if you want to remove scratches from a picture, click on the Recipes tab. A palette drops down from the tab and lets you select from different categories of common image-editing tasks. Removing scratches belongs in the Image Cleanup category, under the item Remove Dust & Scratches. The recipe item describes the steps involved in performing this task and adds an extra layer of help by including a link to menu items.

For example, one of the steps in Remove Dust & Scratches offers, "Select the Rectangular Marquee tool." Normally, this would require that you find and pull down the correct menu from the toolbar, then search for the marquee tool menu item. The software helps by offering a link to the menu item called "Do it for me." Click it and the software will do the choosing for you.

We did not find the Recipes Palette as useful as the Effects and Filters browsers. "Do it for me" does not show how a menu item is chosen; most of the time you do not even know if pressing the link does anything. For what it does, it seems to be no more than a glorified tutorial.

Vector Graphics, Better Text, and Slicing

Version 6 also includes Vector Shapes, which are similar to those in Adobe Illustrator. Vector Shapes allow sharp edges to remain crisp, even when scaling an image. You can use the same Bezier pen tools as in Adobe Illustrator to produce vector data that can be exported in DCS, EPS, PDF, and TIF formats. For example, if a Photoshop document is created with Vector Shapes and then saved as an EPS file, it can be exported to Illustrator as layers, and the vector paths will remain intact. Unfortunately, when an EPS file is reopened in Photoshop, all of the vector data is lost. The biggest advantage to Vector Shapes is that even with large graphics the resulting output will remain clean, unlike with pixel-based graphics. Vector data also consumes much less disk space than pixel-based graphics. Vector Shapes will not replace Illustrator (you would not want to make a complex, multi-layered illustration in Photoshop), but they're a nice addition nonetheless.

Another great feature for those who do not like constructing text in Illustrator and then importing it into Photoshop, is the improved typographical tools. Not only did Adobe add new ligatures and other character options, it also got rid of the clunky text dialog box. Now you can type directly in a document's workspace, which means you can move text quickly without jumping in and out of a separate editing box. This makes both point and paragraph type very easy. You create point type by clicking on the document and typing. You activate paragraph type by click dragging to create a bounding box in which the text wraps automatically. In addition, each kind of type can be converted to the other. Furthermore, Photoshop 6 allows text warping, an editable effect that can manipulate text into a variety of shapes. Unfortunately, Photoshop still lacks the ability to easily create multiple columns of text, which would be handy for laying out single-page designs with large amounts of text.

For Web developers, a Slice Tool has been added to the toolset. Slicing is used to break images into smaller components for quicker display on websites. In the Save for Web dialog box, you can selectively output individual slices and HTML. There is also an option to let Photoshop auto slice by using layers to define the slices. These auto slices adjust as the layers are changed. However, it is still necessary to use Image Ready (bundled with Photoshop 6 in version 3) for GIF animations, rollovers, and image maps. Moreover, for those with a WebDAV (Web-based Distributed

Authoring and Versioning) server, workgroup members can now check files in and out without risk of overwriting one another's work.

Improvements have also been made for 16-bit-per-channel color. For those who prefer to keep their work in high-bit mode as long as possible, the software supports more filters, such as Gaussian Blur, Unsharp Mask, and Dust and Scratches.

Be sure to take a look at Liquefy, an effect for warping, twirling, expanding, contracting, shifting, or reflecting raster portions of an image. Select a brush size and pressure and smear away, or get a bit crazier with tools such as Clockwise Twirl and Shift Pixels. You can use alpha channels as masks to Freeze an area, preventing it from being affected. There is also an option to Reconstruct, which allows a full or partial revert while in the Liquefy dialog box. It is almost as much fun as finger painting, and can be used effectively to exaggerate or de-emphasize portions of photos. Liquefy only works in a separate window, and you cannot view the layer you are liquefying in context, you can only see the target layer.

Chapter 2

Make Older Applications Compatible Windows 3.X and 9X

There are still some stubborn Windows 3.x that behave poorly under Windows 95/98. It is time to teach your program some manners and behave more politely under 32-bit Windows. There is a hidden program in you C:\Windows\System\ directory.

Select Run and type: mkcompat.exe

This will launch a program called Make Compatible. First, click on File, Choose Program. Select the darn program and make your settings It is advisable that you use the Advance Settings for further customization

Make Older Applications Compatible Windows XP

You want to know if all your favorite games are still going to run under Windows XP. Remember what happened when we tried to run games on our Windows 2000 machines? Sometimes we were a little disappointed. Windows 2000 was made more for corporate applications than "Quake," However, true techno-geeks know they do not have to sacrifice death matches for a robust business environment -- at least not anymore.

Windows XP has shown an impressive track record of game compatibility. We ran a number of stand port games, such as "Tiger Woods Golf", "NHL 2001," "Max Payne," and "Unreal" on our Windows XP Professional machine. Some of these games were specifically slated for Windows 95 and 98, and were shown not to work in Windows 2000. The installation in XP was as smooth as silk. The games ran quickly and beautifully -- not a problem in sight.

Some less-sophisticated programs may not run as smoothly, and we found that some older applications, such as the Atari 2600 Classic Game Collection, did not appreciate the Windows XP environment. In this case, you can use the Application Compatibility Wizard, found in the accessories menu. XP includes integrated compatibility layers to mimic older versions of Windows, so if your program does not work in Windows XP, the compatibility wizard will walk you through the process of getting even your favorite DOS games up and running. In this case, we ran the Atari Classic Game Collection in the Windows 95 environment, at 256 colors and 640x480 screen resolution. Then we set XP to always run our Atari application in this environment, and everything was smooth sailing after that.

One final tip about compatibility: Do not run the compatibility wizard if your program appears to be running well in the normal environment, as the wizard will give you an error message. In general, XP has great program compatibility, so you can upgrade your operating system without giving up all your old favorites.

Chapter 3

How to Use the **Fdisk** and **Format Tools**

Before you install your operating system, you must first create a primary partition on the hard drive, drive C: on your computer, and then format a file system on that partition. The Fdisk tool is an MS-DOS-based tool that you can use to prepare or partition a hard drive. You can use the Fdisk tool to create, change, delete, or display current partitions on the hard drive, and then each allocated space on the hard drive (primary partition, extended partition, or logical drive) is assigned a drive letter. Drive C: may contain one extended partition, and a second hard disk may contain a primary or extended partition. An extended partition may contain one or more logical MS-DOS drives.

After you use the Fdisk tool to partition your hard drive, use the Format tool to format those partitions with a file system. The file system File Allocation Table (FAT) allows the hard drive to accept, store, and retrieve data. Windows 95 OEM Service Release 2 (OSR2), Windows 98, Windows 98 Second Edition, Windows

Millennium Edition (Me), and Windows 2000 support the FAT16 and FAT32 file systems. When you run the Fdisk tool on a hard drive that is larger than 512 megabytes (MB), you are prompted to choose one of the following file systems:
FAT16: This file system has a maximum of 2 gigabytes (GB) for each allocated space or drive letter. For example, if you use the FAT16 file system and have a 6-GB hard disk, you can have three drive letters (C, D, and E), each with 2 GB of allocated space.

FAT32: This file system supports drives that are up to 2 terabytes in size and stores files on smaller sections of the hard disk than the FAT16 file system does. This results in more free space on the hard disk. The FAT32 file system does not support drives that are smaller than 512 MB.

When you run the fdisk and format commands, the Master Boot Record (MBR) and file allocation tables are created. The MBR and file allocation tables store the necessary disk geometry that allows hard disk to accept, store, and retrieve data.

MS-DOS Partitioning Summary

Important Considerations Before You Use the Fdisk and Format Tools

Consider the following questions before you use the Fdisk and Format tools:

Is the hard drive new? If not, view the second question. Is this hard disk the only hard drive on your computer master? Or is this hard disk a second hard drive slave? Have you prepared the hard drive by following the manufacturer's instructions? It is important to set the jumpers and cabling according to the role of the hard drive (master or slave).

Have you checked your basic input/output system BIOS to verify that it supports the hard drive or the second hard dive? If not, check the documentation that came with your motherboard, or contact the manufacturer. Typically, the BIOS have an auto detect hard drive setting that configures the drive; However, you should verify this before you continue.

What type of file system do you want to use? You can use either the FAT16 or the FAT32 file systems. Does the hard drive already contain data?

Have you backed up all of your important data? If not, back up your data before you proceed. When you run the fdisk command to create, delete, or change a partition, all of the data on that partition is permanently deleted. Note that you can view current partition information without deleting your data. View the Help file in the MSBackup utility for information about how to use this utility. If you want to use the MSBackup utility with a removable media device.

Note that a backup utility is not included with Windows Me. Does the hard drive have a drive overlay or a disk management program? If your computer uses drive overlay software to enable large hard drive support, do not use the Fdisk tool until you have checked with the software manufacturer.

Do you have the floppy disks or the CD-ROMs that are necessary to reinstall your software? Make sure that you have the software so that you can reinstall your programs after you partition and format your drive. If you purchased an upgrade for a program, make sure that you have the full version of the original program. Many upgrades for programs require a compliance check before you can install the upgraded product. If you cannot find the original floppy disks or CD-ROMs, contact the software manufacturer before you proceed.

Do you have updated device backed up on a device other than the drive that you are about to format and partition? If you have installed an updated device driver for your peripheral devices (for example, modems, printers, and so on), make sure that you back up the new driver on a device other than the drive that you are about to format and partition so that you can reinstall it after you install your operating system.

Do you want to combine multiple extended partitions in one extended partition? If so, view the "How to Repartition and Format the Extended Partition and Logical Drives on a Hard Drive" section in this article.

Do you have a Startup disk? Windows 95, Windows 98, Windows 98 Second Edition, and Windows ME prompt you to create a Startup disk during Setup. If you do not have a Startup disk:

1. Insert a blank floppy disk in the floppy disk drive, drive A.
2. Click Start, point to Settings, click Control Panel, and then double-click Add/Remove Programs.
3. Click Create Disk on the Startup Disk tab.
4. After you create the Startup disk, you should test it. To test the Startup disk, insert it in the floppy disk drive, and then restart your computer. If you are using a Windows 98-based computer, the Startup menu is displayed. If you are using a Windows 95-based computer, a commandprompt is displayed.

Do you need Real-mode CD-ROM support? Some CD-ROM drives require Real-mode device drivers. If you are planning to use Windows 98 on your computer, the Startup disk contains generic, Real-mode ATAPI CD-ROM and Small Computer System Interface (SCSI) drivers that can enable CD-ROM drives after you boot from the Windows 98 Startup disk. Note that these CD-ROM drivers may not work with all CD-ROM drives; they may work as a replacement if the Real-mode CD-ROM drivers that are included with your CD-ROM drive are not available.

NOTE: If you insert your Windows 98 Startup disk, restart your computer; you may not be able to change to the drive letter of your CD-ROM drive. Usually one drive letter ahead of where the drive letter typically resides because there is a random access memory [RAM] drive created by the Startup disk. Because these drivers do not work with your CD-ROM drive. View the documentation that is included with your hard ware, or contact your hard ware manufacturer to obtain the CD-ROM device drivers.

How to Partition and Format a Master Hard Drive

IMPORTANT: If you use the following steps on a hard drive that is not empty, all of the data on that hard drive is permanently deleted.

Chapter 4

How to Partition a Master Hard Drive

To partition a master hard drive, run the fdisk command:

1.   Insert the Startup disk in the floppy disk drive, restart your computer, and then use one of the following methods, depending on your operating system. For a Windows 98, Windows 98 Second Edition, or Windows Me Startup disk:

a.   When the Microsoft Windows 98 Startup menu is displayed, select the Start computer without CD-ROM support menu option, and then press ENTER.
b.   At a commandprompt, type fdisk, and then press ENTER.
c.   View step 2.

For a Windows 9X Startup disk:

d. At a commandprompt, type fdisk, and then press ENTER.
e. View step 2.
f. If your hard disk is larger than 512 MB, you receive the following message:

Your computer has a disk larger than 512 MB. This version of Windows includes improved support for large disks, resulting in more efficient use of disk space on large drives, and allowing disks over 2 GB to be formatted as a single drive.

IMPORTANT: If you enable large disk support and create any new drives on this disk, you will not be able to access the new drive(s) using other operating systems, including some versions of Windows 95 and Windows NT, as well as earlier versions of Windows and MS-DOS. And disk utilities that were not designated explicitly for the FAT32 file system will not be able to work with this disk. If you need to access this disk with other operating systems or older disk utilities, do not enable large drive support.

Do you wish to enable large disk support?

If you want to use the FAT32 file system, press Y and then press ENTER. If you want to use the FAT16 file system, press N, and then press ENTER. For additional information about the FAT32 and FAT16 file systems, click the article numbers below to view the articles in the Microsoft Knowledge Base:

118335 Maximum Partition Size Using FAT16 File System
154997 Description of the FAT32 File System

2. After you press ENTER, the following Fdisk Options menu is displayed:

3. 1. Create DOS partition or Logical DOS Drive

4. 2. Set active partition

5. 3. Delete partition or Logical DOS Drive

6. 4. Display partition information

5. Change current fixed disk drive

Note that option 5 is available only if you have two physical hard drives in the computer.

7. Press 1 to select the Create DOS partition or Logical DOS Drive menu option, and then press ENTER.

8. Press 1 to select the Create Primary DOS Partition menu option, and then press ENTER.
9. After you press ENTER, you receive the following message:

Do you wish to use the maximum available size for primary DOS partition?

After you receive this message, use one of the following methods, depending on the file system that you selected.

For a FAT32 File System

a. If you press Y for the FAT32 file system (in step 2) and you want all of the space on the hard drive to be assigned to drive C, press Y, and then press ENTER.
b. Press ESC, and then press ESC to quit the Fdisk tool and return to a commandprompt.
c. View step 7.

For a FAT16 File System

If you press N for the FAT16 file system (in step 2), you can accept the default 2 GB size for the partition size, or you can customize the size of the partition.

To accept the default partition size:

d. If you want the first 2 GB on the hard drive to be assigned to drive C, press Y, and then press ENTER.

e. Press ESC to return to the Options menu, and then view step d in the following "To customize the partition size" section.

To customize the partition size:

f. If you want to customize the size of the partitions (drive letters) on the hard drive, press N, and then press ENTER.

g. A dialog box is displayed in which you can type the size that you want for the primary partition in MB or percent of disk space. Note that for computers that are running either Windows 98 or Windows Me, Microsoft recommends that you make the primary partition at least 500 MB in size. Type the size of the partition that you want to create, and then press ENTER.

h. Press ESC to return to the Options menu.

i. To assign drive letters to the additional space on the hard drive, press 1, and then press ENTER.

j. Press 2 to select the Create Extended DOS Partition menu option, and then press ENTER.

k. You receive a dialog box that is displays the maximum space that is available for the extended partition. You can adjust the size of the partition or use the default size. Note that the default maximum space is recommended, However, you can divide the space between multiple drive letters. Type the amount of space that you want, press ENTER, and then press ESC.

l. The Create Logical DOS Drive(s) in the Extended DOS Partition menu is displayed. This menu that you can use to assign the remaining hard drive space to the additional drive letters. Type the amount of space that you want to assign to the next drive letter in the Enter logical drive size in Mbytes or percent of disk space (%) box, and then press ENTER.

m. A table that lists the drive letter that you created and the amount of space on that drive is displayed. If there is free space on the hard drive, it is displayed near the bottom of the table. Repeat steps e through g until you receive the following message:

All available space in the Extended DOS Partition is assigned to local drives.

n. After you receive this message, press ESC to return to the Options menu.
o. To activate the partition from which you plan to boot (usually drive C), press 2 to select the Set active partition menu option, and then press ENTER.
p. When you receive the following message, press 1, and then press ENTER:

Enter the number of the partition you want to make active.

q. Press ESC, and then press ESC to quit the Fdisk tool and return to a command prompt, and then view the following "How to Format a Hard Drive" section in this article.

Chapter 5

How to Format a Hard Drive

After you create the partitions, you must format the partitions:

1. Restart your computer with the Startup disk in the floppy disk drive.

NOTE: If you are using a Windows 95 Startup disk, a command prompt is displayed and you can skip to step 2. If you are using a Windows 98, Windows 98 Second Edition, or Windows Me Startup disk, select the Start computer without CD-ROM support menu option when the Windows 98 Startup menu is displayed.

2. When a command prompt is displayed, type format c: /s, and then press ENTER. This command transfers the system files and should only be used when you format drive C (or your "active" drive). For all other partitions, type format drive (where drive is the letter of the partition that you want to format).

NOTE: If you receive a "Bad command" or "Bad file name" error message, you may need to extract the Format.com tool to your boot disk. To do this, type the following command at a command prompt, and then press ENTER:

extract ebd.cab format.com

After the Format.com tool is extracted to your boot disk, type format c: /s, a at command prompt to format your active partition, or type format drive: if you want to format a partition that is not your active partition.

2. When you successfully run the Format.com tool, you receive the following message:

WARNING, ALL DATA ON NON-REMOVABLE DISK DRIVE C: WILL BE LOST!
Proceed with Format?

3. Press Y, and then press ENTER to format drive C.

4. After the format procedure is finished, you receive the following message:

Volume label (11 characters, ENTER for none)?

NOTE: This is an optional feature that you can use to type a name for the drive. Either you can type an 11-character name for the drive, or you can leave it blank by pressing ENTER.

Chapter 6

How to Repartition and Format a Slave Hard Drive

How to Repartition a Slave Hard Drive

If you want to add a second hard drive (slave drive) to your computer, you need to make sure that the jumpers on both the master (original) and slave (new drive) are set according to the manufacturer's instructions first so that your computer can detect the hard drives. Verify that your hard ware is installed correctly, and then follow these steps:

1. Click Start, point to Run, and then type command (Note that the cmd command only works on Windows 2000-based computers).
2. At a commandprompt, type fdisk, and then press ENTER. The following menu is displayed:

3. 1. Create DOS partition or Logical DOS Drive

4. 2. Set active partition

5. 3. Delete partition or Logical DOS Drive

6. 4. Display partition information

5. Change current fixed disk drive

Note that menu option 5 is available only if you have two physical hard dives on your computer.

7. Press 5, and then press ENTER. When you do this, the selection changes from the physical disk 1 (master) to the physical disk 2 (slave).

8. Press 1 to select the Create DOS partition or Logical DOS Drive menu option, press ENTER, press 2 to select the Create Extended DOS Partition menu option, and then press ENTER. When you make your slave drive an extended MS-DOS partition, your drive letters does not change. For example, if the first drive contains partition C and partition D, your slave drive becomes D unless you set the slave drive as an extended partition. If you skip this step and just create another primary MS-DOS partition for the slave drive, the new drive becomes drive D and what used to be drive D, changes to drive E.

9. You can partition the slave drive to make other logical drives just as you did with the original master drive. If your computer cannot detect the new drive, you may need to add the following line to your Config.sys file, where drive is a letter that is greater than the last drive letter on the computer (including the CD-ROM drive):

Lastdrive=drive

10. After you finish using the Fdisk tool, format the new partitions so that you can use them. After you press ESC to quit the Fdisk tool, restart your computer to start Windows.

How to Format a Slave Hard Drive

To format your new partition or partitions, use one of the following methods, depending on your file system. For a FAT16 file system:

1. Double-click My Computer, right-click the partition that you just created, click Format, click Full, and then click Start.
2. After the format, procedure is complete, click OK to close the dialog box.
For a FAT32 file system:

1. Click Start, point to Programs, point to Accessories, and point to System Tools, click Drive Converter (FAT32), and then click Next.
2. In the Drives box, click the drive that you want to convert to the FAT32 file system.
3. Click Next, and then click OK.
4. Click Next, click Next, and then click Next again.
5. When the conversion procedure is finished, click Finish.
NOTE: Do not use the /s switch that you used when you set up drive C. All you need to do is to format the drive or drives so that you can use them (for example, if you created two new drive letters, you need to format both drives).

For information about how to repartition the extended partition and logical drives, view the following "How to Repartition and Format the Extended Partition and Logical Drives of a Hard Drive" section in this article.
Back to the top

How to Repartition and Format the Extended Partition and Logical Drives of a Hard Drive

Use the steps in this section to resize or combine your extended partition and logical drives. Make sure that you have a reliable backup of any important data that you have on your extended partition and logical drives before you proceed. If you want to combine your entire hard drive in one partition, use the steps in the

"How to Partition and Format a Master Hard Drive" section in this article.

Chapter 7

How to Repartition the Extended Partition and the Logical Drives

NOTE: When you use this method, two or more partitions are left on your hard drive, a primary partition (usually drive C) and an extended partition. Even if you use the FAT32 file system, there is an 8-GB partition limitation unless you obtain a BIOS upgrade that fully supports interrupt 13 extensions.

153550 Hard Drive Limited to 8-GB Partition
If you have a hard drive that is larger than 8 GB and you are not using disk overlay program or disk management software, you need to partition and format the space that is remaining after you create each 8-GB partition:

1.   Place the Startup disk in your floppy disk drive, restart your computer, and then use one of the following methods, depending on your operating system. For a Windows 98, Windows 98 Second Edition, or Windows Me Startup disk:

a.   When the Microsoft Windows 98 Startup menu is displayed, select the Start computer without CD-ROM support menu option, and then press ENTER.
b.   At a commandprompt, type fdisk, and then press ENTER.
c.   Go to step 2.

From a Windows 9X Startup disk:

d.   At a commandprompt, type fdisk, and then press ENTER.

- Go to step 2.

2. If your hard disk is larger than 512 MB, you receive the following message:

Your computer has a drive larger than 512 MB. This version of Windows includes improved support for large drives, resulting in more efficient use of disk space on large drives, and allowing drives over 2 GB to be formatted as a single drive.

IMPORTANT: If you enable large disk support and create any new drives on this disk, you will not be able to access the new drive(s) using other operating systems, including some versions of Windows 9X and Windows NT, as well as earlier versions of Windows and MS-DOS. And disk utilities that were not designated explicitly for the FAT32 file system will not be able to work with this disk. If you need to access this disk with other operating systems or older disk utilities, do not enable large drive support.

Do you wish to enable large disk support (Y/N)?

If you want to use the FAT32 file system, press Y and then press ENTER. If you want to use the FAT16 file system, press N, and then press ENTER. For additional information about the FAT32 and FAT16 file systems, click the article numbers below to view the articles in the Microsoft Knowledge Base:

118335 Maximum Partition Size Using FAT16 File System
154997 Description of the FAT32 File System

3. After you press ENTER, the following Fdisk Options menu is displayed:

4. 1. Create DOS partition or Logical DOS Drive

5. 2. Set active partition

34

6. 3. Delete partition or Logical DOS Drive

7. 4. Display partition information

8. 5. Change current fixed disk drive

9. (this option is only available if you

have two physical hard drives in the computer)

10. Press 3, and then press ENTER. The following menu is displayed:

11. 1. Delete Primary DOS Partition

12. 2. Delete Extended DOS Partition

13. 3. Delete Logical DOS Drive(s) in the Extended DOS Partition

4. Delete Non-DOS Partition

14. Press 3, and then press ENTER.
15. The Delete Logical DOS Drive(s) in the Extended DOS Partition screen is displayed with a chart that describes the attriHowever, es of your hard drive, as shown in the following example.

D	Volume Labe	Mby	System	Usa
D:	(User Defined)	2047	FAT16	100%
E:	(User Defined)	2047	FAT16	100%

F:	(User Defined)	2047	FAT16	100%
G:	(User Defined)	2047	FAT16	100%
H:	(User Defined)	2047	FAT32	17%
I:	(User Defined)	1498	UNKNOWN	13%

16. Total Extended DOS Partition size is XXX Mbytes (1 MByte = 1048576 bytes).
17. WARNING! Data in a deleted Logical DOS Drive will be lost.

18. What drive do you want to delete? Type the letter for the drive that you want to delete, and then press ENTER.

19. When you are prompted to type the volume label for the drive, type the volume label if the drive has a volume label.

NOTE: You must type the exact label or press ENTER if there is no volume label. If you type an incorrect label name, you receive the following message:

Volume label does not match.
Enter Volume Label?

If you type the correct volume label, you receive the following message:

Are you sure (Y/N)?

The default answer to this message is N. You must press Y, and then press ENTER to delete the drive. The words "Drive deleted" are displayed in the chart next to the drive letter that you deleted.

20. Repeat steps 3 through 7 until you have deleted all of the drives that you want to delete. When you are finished, press ESC. If you remove all of the logical drives, you receive a "No logical drives defined" message and a chart of drive letters that you changed or deleted. Press ESC to continue.

NOTE: If you want to resize the logical drive or drives by making them larger or smaller, do this now. If you want to remove the extended partition, view step 11.

21. Press 1 to select the Create DOS partition or Logical DOS Drive menu option from the Fdisk Options menu, press 3 to select the Create Logical DOS Drive(s) in the Extended DOS Partition menu option from the Create DOS Partition or Logical DOS Drive menu, and then press ENTER. When you do this, you receive a "Verifying drive integrity" message with a percentage-complete counter.

NOTE: When you use this step, the extended partition is not

deleted, only the logical drive or drives in the extended partition are deleted. You do not need to remove the extended partition to resize the logical drives. For example, if you have one logical drive in the extended partition and you want to make two logical drives, delete the logical drive and create two logical drives in the extended partition first. Note that you are still limited to the total space in the extended partition.

21. After the drive verification procedure is finished, you receive the following message:

Total Extended DOS Partition size is XXX Mbytes (1 MByte = 1048576 bytes)

Maximum space available for logical drive is XXX Mbytes (X%)

Enter logical drive size in Mbytes or percent of disk space (%).

The "maximum Mbytes available" is the default size; however, you can change the number if you type the number for the partition size that you want to create, and then pressing ENTER. Press ESC, press ESC to quit the Fdisk tool and return to a commandprompt, and then view step 11.

22. If you want to remove the extended MS-DOS partition, press ESC to return to the Fdisk Options menu. Press 3 to select the Delete DOS Partition or Logical DOS Drive menu option, press ENTER, press 2 to select the Delete Extended DOS Partition menu option, and then press ENTER.

23. The screen shows the current fixed disk drive and information about it. The extended partition is listed in the Type column. For example:

24. Partition Status Type Volume Label   Mbytes System Usage

25. C: 1 A   PRI DOS   (your label) 1200 FAT16 50%

26. 2   EXT DOS   (your label) 1200 UNKNOWN 50%

27. Total disk space is 2400 Mbytes (1 MByte = 1048576 bytes)

You also receive the following warning message:

WARNING! Data in the deleted Extended DOS Partition will be lost.

Do you wish to continue (Y/N)?

28. Press Y, and then press ENTER to delete the partition. You receive the following message:

Extended DOS Partition deleted
Press ESC to continue

NOTE: If you try to delete your extended MS-DOS partition before you remove all of the logical drives, you receive the following error message:

Cannot delete Extended DOS Partition while logical drives exist.

If you receive this error message, repeat steps 3 through 6, and then follow steps 9 and 10 to delete the extended MS-DOS partition.

The Fdisk Options menu is displayed. If you leave disk space unpartitioned on your hard drive, Windows may not display the full size of your hard drive, only the amount of space that is available.

IMPORTANT: After you change the Fdisk options or delete partitions, the data that was on the partition is deleted and cannot be retrieved. Be very sure that you understand this procedure before you attempt to follow it. If you want to start with a clean configuration or if you want to redo your current configuration, back up everything that is important to you before you use the Fdisk tool.

29. If you want to use the unpartitioned space on your hard drive, you must format the drives. When you successfully run the Format.com utility, you receive the following message:

WARNING, ALL DATA ON NON-REMOVABLE DISK DRIVE X: WILL BE LOST!
Proceed with Format (Y/N)?

Press Y, and then press ENTER to format the drive.

30. After the format procedure is finished, you receive the following message:

Volume label (11 characters, ENTER for none)?

NOTE: This is an optional feature that you can use to type a name for the hard drive. You can either type an 11-character name for the drive, or leave it blank and press ENTER.

Chapter 8

Checking Drives With My Computer general

Need a simple report or check on your drive? Go to My Computer, right-click on any hard drive and select Properties. There will be a pie chart report on your drive's free space and used space. For your information, checking drive space on Windows might not be accurate if you have Norton Protection installed because Windows will just refer those files are "free space". Go to DOS Prompt and the simple DIR command will be enough to report accurate free disk space. For further understanding, 1 megabyte is not 1000 kb However, 1024 kb because computers only count with the power of two.

Move on to the Tools tab. There will be a small report on when your drive was last diagnosed will the system tools. Useful if you have forgotten when was your last time you scanned or defragment your drive.

Chapter 9

Looking At System Information

Microsoft has finally pumped up the System Information tools and added into the System Tools folder. It enables you to check whether your CPU is a genuine Intel chip, your FAT system, RAM and more. You can also check for conflicts with it. You are IRC and DMA settings can be viewed here. However, on top of all, there is a bunch of very useful hidden tools like Dr. Watson, Registry Checker, and System File Checker. This tool is very useful to keep your system running on good condition

Chapter 10

Microsoft PowerToys

▪ PowerToys will only work with US-English regional settings.

Just look at your PowerToy choices:

Open CommandWindow Here

This PowerToy adds an "Open CommandWindow Here" context menu option on file system folders, giving you a quick way to open a commandwindow (cmd.exe) pointing at the selected folder.

Alt-Tab Replacement

With this PowerToy, in addition to seeing the icon of the application window you are switching to, you will also see a preview of the page. This helps particularly when multiple sessions of an application are open.

Tweak UI

This PowerToy gives you access to system settings that are not exposed in the Windows XP default user interface, including mouse settings, Explorer settings, taskbar settings, and more.

Version 2.10 requires Windows XP Service Pack 1 or Windows Server 2003.

Power Calculator

With this PowerToy, you can graph and evaluate functions as well as perform many different types of conversions.

Image Resizer

This PowerToy enables you to resize one or many image files with a right-click.

CD Slide Show Generator

With this PowerToy, you can view images burned to a CD as a slide show. The Generator works down level on Windows 9x machines as well.

Virtual Desktop Manager

Manage up to four desktops from the Windows taskbar with this PowerToy.

Taskbar Magnifier

Use this PowerToy to magnify part of the screen from the taskbar.

HTML Slide Show Wizard

This wizard helps you create an HTML slide show of your digital pictures, ready to place on your Web site.

Web cam Timershot

This PowerToy lets you take pictures at specified time intervals from a Web cam connected to your computer and save them to a location that you designate.

Chapter 11

MS Paint

MS Paint is a very simple-to-use graphics application. Mainly it is used for drawing diagrams or electronic painting. If you are doing the Education course next term, you will need to familiarize yourself with it However; even if you are not it can be a very useful addition to your transferable skills.

The first thing we are going to do with it is to edit the image of the milk bottle.
Make sure the picture is selected in Word and choose Edit: Copy
Start the Paint program; choose Start: Programs: Accessories: Paint.
In the Paint window, choose Edit: Paste. If you get a message about re-sizing the area, say yes!

Click on the Eraser Button near the top left of the window.
We are going to rub out part of the image.
Notice the choice of eraser sizes offered. Choose the largest for the moment.

Uses the erasers by dragging the cursor over the image with the left mouse Button held down and try to round off the bottom of the milk bottle. (Hint: experiment with different
eraser sizes or you could even try the airbrush tool to create an eater effect.)

Note that this will be a file of type '.bmp' (short for bitmap). This is the type of file produced by Paint. You could look up bitmap on the web if you want to know more!

Go back to your Word document and delete the original milk bottle picture. Just select it and hit 'delete'. Now insert the new version (i.e. 'milk.bmp') by choosing Insert: Picture: From File and then navigate to the file as usual.

When the image is inserted, make sure it is formatted to 'float over the text'.
Making sure the image is selected; choose Edit: Copy and then Edit Paste to make a copy of it. Move the copy away from the original and reduce it to about a quarter of its previous size. Now copy the copy several times and position the copies around the page in a kind of random pattern.
(Save your document).

Chapter 12

Creating Your Own Icons

So, you want to create your own icons? Actually custom icons are easier than you thought. First, open up paint. Next, select Image AttriHowever, es. Then change both width and height to 32

Paint your new icon and make sure you leave the background white. Next, save the file with an .ico extension. Now, to use your own icons, right-click any shortcut and select properties. Select the Shortcut tab and click on the Advance Settings Button. Type in the full path of where your icon is situated. You can now use your own icon!

Chapter 13

Custom Clipboard Tips general

Are you annoyed when the new Office Clipboard toolbar pops up unexpectedly?

Adjusting an undocumented Registry key lets you choose when to use the Office Clipboard. Search for the key HKEY_CURRENT_USER Software Microsoft Office 9.0 Common General, and add a new DWORD value, AcbControl. Change its setting from 0 (the default) to 1; this disables the Clipboard toolbar triggers.

Clipboard copying

This is a super copy-in addition;-paste feature within Word, Excel, PowerPoint, and Access. The clipboard holds 24 items.

1. Copy or cut an item from any Office program.
2. Open another file.
3. Move cursor to location to paste item.
4. Click Edit Office Clipboard.
5. Right-click on item and click Clipboard Paste.

Try copying and pasting text

Put your cursor on this sentence, and drag it across the text with the left mouse Button held down. This will highlight the text you want to copy. With the text highlighted, you have three ways to copy:

1. Choose Edit, and then Copy from your browser menu.
2. On the other hand , click the right mouse Button and choose Copy from the drop-down menu.

3. Alternatively, press the CTRL key and the C key simultaneously.

The text should now be saved to the Clipboard. The Clipboard is a little program that holds data, such as text and graphics, between programs.

Now open a text editor, such as Word. Make sure your cursor is in the document. There are three ways to paste the text from the clipboard into your document:

1. Choose Edit, then Paste from your browser menu.
2. On the other hand, click the right mouse Button and choose Paste from the drop-down menu.
3. Or, press the CTRL and the V key simultaneously.

You have just copied and pasted.

How to View the Clipboard's Contents

The Clipboard temporarily holds data while you move it from one program to another. You can see what you have pasted onto the clipboard by using the Clipboard Viewer accessory, which is available on Windows 95 and 98 However, is not always installed. Here is how to find out if Clipboard Viewer is installed on your system:

-   Click on the Start Button.
-   Click on Programs, then Accessories, then System Tools.

If the viewer is installed you should see it within the system tools.

If Clipboard Viewer is not installed, it is easy to do:

-   Click the Start Button, then Settings, then Control Panels, and then Add/Remove.

- Click on the Windows Set Up tab.
- Scroll down until you see the Clipboard Viewer. Click on the program name, so that a check appears in the box next to it.

You will have to restart your computer to activate the Clipboard Viewer. Once it is installed, you can use it to see what you have pasted to the Clipboard, and how the contents change, as you copy and paste.

Chapter 14

Use Hotmail With Outlook Express

Users of Outlook Express, which comes with Microsoft's Internet Explorer, have noticed that they can download and send mail using a Hotmail account. Hotmail users can get the best of both worlds: the convenience of Web-based email accessible from anywhere with the power and flexibility of an email client like Outlook Express.

If you have a Hotmail account, you will add it to Outlook Express as you would any other email account.

1. Use the Accounts item under the Tools menu.
2. Create an entry for an account as usual using the Add Button.
3. When you specify an address ending in @hotmail.com, OE will recognize it as a Web-based account and give you a number of Web-specific options, including downloading your Hotmail folder structure.

If you do not have a Hotmail account, you can use Outlook Express to create one.

Go to the Create New Account... menu item under the Tools menu.

After creating a Hotmail account in OE, you will be able to use it like any other POP mail account: for retrieving email from Hotmail and storing it on your local hard drive, using OE's sophisticated filtering capabilities, and so on.

Sync Folders

How do you synchronize your mail when you have a notebook and a desktop PC However, you do not connect via an Exchange server?

Check Microsoft's Office Update Web site (officeupdate.microsoft.com) for the add-in Outlook Sync Folders (not yet available). This utility lets you transfer changed data between two Personal Folders (*.PST) files without copying the entire large file each time.

Microsoft will also be posting an easy to use backup program for PST files to make it far easier to keep backups of mail etc on your PC.

Flagging E-mail

Outlook makes it easy for you to mark up e-mails that you may want to go back to later.

By right clicking on an e-mail in your inbox and then clicking on the "Flag For Follow Up" option you get a number of different choices, they include "Follow Up", "Reply", "Forward " and "Call" by selecting the appropriate one you will flag the e-mail. A small flag will appear next to the e-mail on the left. And you can then go back to it later on when you wish to continue with your reply or whatever it is you flagged it for.

To clear the flag just right click on the flagged mail and then "Clear Flag" or if you have followed up on your flagged mail just click on "Flag Complete"

Creating A Web Calendar

Outlook offers some very cool new features one is that you can share your Outlook calendar with other people even if you do not have access to an Exchange server.

Switch to the Calendar folder and choose File, Save As Web Page. Choose the start and end dates you want to publish and specify whether you want to include details about each appointment from the Notes box. Give the calendar a title, specify a file location, and click on Save. Although you cannot save directly to a Web server using this technique, you can save the calendar as a file and then publish it to a Web server. The result is a slick, frame-based page that lets you click on individual dates in the month view at left and see details in the frame on the right.

Plain Text E-Mail Settings For Certain Contacts

If there is a particular person in your contacts list that would rather you did not mail him/her HTML or enhanced e-mail you can set them to receive only plain text e-mail.

Click on CONTACTS and then click on the appropriate name in your address book. Just below their e-mail address will be a tag, which you can tick to make sure they only get your e-mail in Plain Text.

Chapter 15

FrontPage general

Cleaning Out FrontPage Temp Files

This is just a simple tip for those of you who have FrontPage and do not realize that it does not tend to clean out the Temporary files that it creates in its directory. This tip can help you free up quite a lot of space.

Go to your C:\Program Files\Microsoft FrontPage directory and then enter the Temporary folder that is in that directory. Here you will find hundreds of temporary files that are no longer needed However, do not get deleted. Click on EDIT | SELECT ALL and then Right click all the files and press DELETE.

Next just empty your recycle bin and all the files will depart.

Using Arrow Keys With Your Document

The arrow keys on your Keyboard are a good way to navigate around your document, especially when it is first opened in the FrontPage Editor. Remember if you hold the Ctrl key down when you press the up or down arrow keys, you will jump by a paragraph at a time. And Ctrl-End will take you to the very end of your document, and Ctrl-Home will take you to the very beginning.

Opening Links In Sized Windows

The following tip describes how you can create a link that will Open in a New Window using JavaScript. There are three variations shown below. You can use the on Click event or the on Mouse Over event. The brackets [] indicate the optional entries.

The JavaScript used is in the form of: On Click = [window].open("URL", "windowName", ["windowOptions"])

On Mouse Over = [window].open("URL", "windowName", ["windowOptions"])

Create your link like any other link. You can use a Text link or Graphic link In HTML View edit the link and add one of the following after the <a href="URL" and before the > in the link.

On Click = [window].open("URL", "windowName", ["windowOptions"]) for an onClick event. On Mouse Over = [window].open("URL", "windowName", ["windowOptions"]) for an on Mouse Over event.

NOTE: In the examples, newwindow.htm is this page, and samplewindow.htm is the page opened in the New Window. You can replace on Click with on Mouse Over to open a new window when the mouse passes over the link.

How Can I Change Text Hidden In Tags In Multiple Documents At Once?

Find and Replace feature only looks for text that would be displayed in the browser. However, you can create a macro in MS Word that will make the change you want; you can then save the document back as html.

1. Change all of the extensions to .TXT in the Windows Explorer (not FrontPage's). (This step may not be necessary if you are using Word.)
2. Record the steps needed to make the change you want, and then save the file as .TXT.
3. Save the macro as AUTOOPEN in your normal .dot (Word's base template).

4. Select all of the files and open them at the same time. (As soon as it opens each of the files, Word executes the macro.)

5. In the Windows explorer, change all of the extensions back to .HTM.

6. In the AUTOOPEN macro, delete the text between "Sub MAIN" AND "End Sub". (Use Tools|Macro|Edit). Otherwise, the macro will execute every time you open Word.

What Does The File Extension *.SHTML Mean?

In most systems, the .shtml file extension identifies an HTML page that contains Server Side Include (SSI) directives (include another file, show date last modified, and so on). Server software must parse files looking for SSI directives, and then carry them out). This would really slow down the httpd server if it had to do this for all files; therefore, the special .shtml designation.

We use the .shtml extension for most of our pages on this website.

Create A Hovering CSS Background

Have you ever visited the GeoCities Web site using a DHTML-compatible browser such as Internet Explorer 4.0 or Navigator 4.0? Did you notice the little logo hovering over the page in the lower-right corner? When you scroll up and down, it keeps its position. That trick involves a background image effect you can get by using Cascading Style Sheets (CSS). With FrontPage 98 it is a cinch to do:

1. In the FrontPage Editor, right-click the current page and then select Page Properties from the pop-up menu.

2. In the Page Properties dialog box under the General tab, click the Style Button. On the Style property sheet, select the Colors tab.

3. In the Background Image field, either type in the location of the image you want to use or click the Browse Button to locate it with the file selector.

4. Next, direct your attention to the four drop-down fields to the right of the property sheet. In the Attachment field, select Fixed. This will keep the graphic in a set position on the page. (Otherwise, it will scroll along with everything else.)
5. In the Repeat field, select No Repeat so that the image will not tile over the whole page.
6. Finally, in the Vertical and Horizontal position fields, select where you want your image to be located on the page. For our example, select Bottom for vertical and Right for horizontal.

After you click a couple of OK Button s, you will see your image tiled in the background of the current page in the FrontPage Editor. Do not worry; you did not mess up anything. It is just that the Editor does not let you preview DHTML content, so you will have to switch over to Preview mode (or preview the page in your browser) to see the trick in action.

Simple Redirection

By using <META refresh>, you can automatically redirect a user's browser to your new Web location. In FrontPage, it is easy. Just open your home page in the FrontPage Editor, right-click the page, and select Page Properties from the pop-up menu. Click the Custom Tab and then the Add Button located to the right of the System Variables section. For this example, type refresh for the Name. Then enter the following for the Value: 5; URL=http://www.microsoft.com/frontpage/default.asp For your own use, change the 5 to the number of seconds you want the browser to wait until it refreshes, and change the URL to your new location. When a visitor arrives at your old home page, their browser will wait for the specified number of seconds and then automatically redirect them to the new URL.

Create Quick Links

Select the target text you want to make into a bookmark by right clicking it. Then drag the text to wherever you want the link created. When you release the mouse Button, select Link Here from the pop-up menu. FrontPage will automatically turn your target text into a bookmark and create a link to that bookmark at the location you specified. However, what about external links? While browsing the Web, you may come across a cool site you would like to link to using FrontPage. Traditionally, this would mean typing in a text description for the link, selecting that text, using the Insert/Hyperlink menu, and typing in the URL If you are using Internet Explorer, however, it does not have to be so time consuming. You can just click the small IE page icon located in the far left of IE's Address Bar and drag it into the FrontPage Editor. FrontPage will then automatically create a link to that page at that cursor location and use the page's title as the name for the link. (You can also use this trick in Netscape Navigator by dragging the link icon that is to the left of the location box from Navigator to FrontPage.) And if Internet Explorer fills your entire screen and is on top of the FrontPage Editor, you can drag the page icon onto the Windows taskbar first and hover over the FrontPage Editor symbol until the program is brought to the front. (Unfortunately, this little trick does not work with Netscape Navigator.)

Make A Quick Global Change

If you have any kind of common information that you want to display on more than one page on your site, create a variable for it. Variables act as placeholders--when it comes time to change the information, all you need to do is modify the associated variable, and FrontPage automatically updates every instance of that variable, saving you the headache of performing the same task over and over again. Suppose you want to include your company's phone number on multiple pages in your site (or even multiple locations on a single page) and make it easy to edit in the future. Simply select Tools/Web Settings in FrontPage Explorer click the Parameters tab, and then the Add Button. In the Name field, type

Company Phone. In the Value field, enter your phone number. Click OK twice, and your variable is set. Now open the FrontPage Editor by double-clicking the pages in your Web that you want to include your company's phone number. Move the cursor to the location in which you would like the number to appear, and then select Insert/FrontPage Component. Now choose the Substitution component and click OK. From the drop-down list that appears, select your Company Phone variable and click OK. Your company's phone number will appear on the page and take on any formatting characteristics you have set for that area. Now, if your area code or entire phone number changes, you can simply go back to the Web Settings dialog box and type in a new value for the Company Phone variable. FrontPage automatically updates all occurrences of that variable in your site.

Simply Adding Banner Services Code

If you have joined one of the online banner swapping services like the Internet Link Exchange (there is an ILE banner at the top of this page) or any other banner service, you will already know that they give you some HTML code to add to your pages. The best way to insert the code is by using the HTML Markup.

First copy the code that you got via email or from the banner services website, and then open the page you want the banner to appear in the FrontPage Editor. Select FrontPage Component... from the Insert menu, and then double click on Insert HTML. Paste the banner code into the window (you will have to use Ctrl-V to paste). After you click OK, you will find a small yellow box in your document with an exclamation point in it. If you want the banner to appear centered on the page simply click the yellow box, then click the Center Button on the toolbar.

Adding Meta Tags In FrontPage

a   Title - Entered on the General tab

- o Some search engines will display the text located in the Title Tag when your web page is listed in a search
- o Title tags show up in people's bookmarks
- o Should be between 5 and 20 words
- o Use your Company/Organization name plus keywords
- o Cut & Paste your Title in HTML view so it is just under the \<head\> tag.

b   Description (Meta Tag) - Use Add for User Variable on the Custom tab

- o Some search engines display this as the summary of your Web page
- o Not all search engines use this tag
- o Try to limit your Description to less than 200 characters.

c   Keywords (Meta Tag) - Use Add for User Variable on the Custom tab

- o One way to maximize the usefulness of keywords is to incorporate singular and plural cases of words as well as active and passive verbs
- o Do not excessively repeat keywords tag as search engines may penalize you for this
- o Not all search engines use this tag
- o Try to limit your keywords between 800 and 1,000 characters
- o do not repeat words more than 3 times

Avoid using the HTTP-EQUIV REFRESH tag because many search engines will not index the page. Also, make sure there is adequate text on your page so search engines like Excite will index it properly. Excite is one of those that do not use Meta Tags.

The best thing to do is to submit each page to the search engines, despite them not saying so.

The Screen Resolutions For Various Other Platforms Are

Resolution	Windows PC	Macintosh
Low	640 x 480	470 x 300
Medium	800 x 600	470 x 430
High	1024 x 768	470 x 600

Web TV	
Colors	216
Scroll bar	None
Width	544
Height	Varies -- reformats the page to fit with 18-point serif font

How Do I Get Rid Of Underlines For Links?

As an HTML author, you can make links appear without underlined text using the STYLE tag. You do this by turning off text decoration for anchor elements. An example of the syntax is:

<STYLE>

<!--

A: link{text-decoration: none

}

-->

</STYLE>

You may want to have some tags that format the text used for links other than the STYLE tag since many browsers do not support the STYLE attriHowever, e (Internet Explorer, Netscape and Oprah

Do). There are many examples of CSS Style tags throughout this site and on our many other websites.

How Can I Control In Which A Document Is Displayed From A Link?

If you are creating a link from a document in one frame and want it to display a document in another frame, specify the Target Frame in the link's Hypertext Properties.

You may want to use "_self" as the default target frame in the link properties if you are jumping from a link that appears in the frame where you want the next document to appear. Certain strings have special meaning when used as targets. These are:

_self: The document will be opened in the same frame you clicked in.

_top: The document will be opened in the full browser window. This makes the display a single pane again.

_blank: The document will be opened in a new window.

_parent: The "Parent" frame set of the current frame will become a single frame where the document will be displayed.

If you are having problems with a link, you may want to check the spelling of the Target Frame and of the Default Frame in the document being displayed and whether the case is correct; for example, "main" instead of "MAIN." You can use Notepad to open the document in which you defined your frameset to check the spelling.

Bring Users Back With A Button

In FrontPage, you can easily create a custom Back Button by using one of the many FrontPage Components available in the FrontPage Editor. Just position the cursor on the page where you want the Button to appear and select Insert/FrontPage Component. Choose Insert HTML from the Component list and click OK. In the Insert HTML dialog box, enter the following:

<FORM><INPUT type="Button" value="Back" onClick="history.go (-1)"></FORM>
Click OK again, and you have your very own Back Button. Your visitors will thank you for it.

Take Your Web With You

Web builders are not just working from their offices anymore. They are taking their work with them on the road and offline. If you occasionally need to take your Web work where an Internet connection will not go, FrontPage's Publish feature is just what you need. It creates a disk-based copy of your site (in a folder on your local hard drive) so you can work on it while you are on the road. To publish your site to your local file system, click the Publish Button in FrontPage Explorer. In the Publish dialog box, click the More Webs Button. Then type in the full path where you want your site located. If the folder does not exist, FrontPage will offer to create it. When you are finished, you can simply copy the new folder to a disk and take it with you wherever you go. Another benefit is that you can now post the site to any Web server, no matter what type it is. Note, however, that your FrontPage Components will not work unless the server has the FrontPage Server Extensions installed. These Components include the Search form, Form Results (the default form-handler), the Discussion form, and the Registration form.

Chapter 16

Office general

Make the Most of Microsoft Office

The latest offering in the world of suites is Microsoft's Office, and it is a doozy. More finely interconnected than its predecessor Office, Office also adds a new email/personal planner component.

How do you actually use all this stuff once you have gone down and shelled out the big bucks for Office? Well, that is where we can help.

However, you say, how do you actually use all this stuff once you have gone down and shelled out the big bucks for it? Well, that is where we can help. Settle in for an extensive introduction to Office and the individual suitemates-- Word, Excel, PowerPoint, and Outlook.

The Stand port edition of Microsoft Office includes new versions of Word, Excel, the PowerPoint presentation graphics program, and the Outlook desktop information manager. Outlook-- the new member of the suite-- integrates email, scheduling, contacts, tasks, and access to documents.

This article introduces you to all the programs that make up the Office suite and provides detailed instructions for getting started making documents, spreadsheets, and presentations. We also have a resource list of related Office links.

There are four different editions of MS Office, and the differences are detailed at the Microsoft site. We will focus here on the Stand port edition for Windows 95 and assume that the suite has already been installed. Much of the information here still applies if you are using a stand -alone version of Word or Excel.

Common Tasks

Many tasks are similar across all the Office applications. Functions like opening and closing the different programs, creating a new file or opening, closing and saving an existing file, and getting online help work exactly the same in Word, Excel, PowerPoint, and Outlook. This section walks you through the steps to perform these common tasks.

Opening and closing programs

There are several ways to open and close the programs that make up Office. Probably the easiest way to open any of the programs is to use the Start Button on the Taskbar (the bar across the bottom of the screen in Windows 95). To do this, click on the Start Button, this brings up the Start Menu. Then move your mouse up and click on the word "Programs" in this pop-up menu. Now you should see a list of installed programs, which includes Word, Excel, PowerPoint, and Outlook.

Whenever a program is open in Windows 95, there will be a Button for it on the Taskbar.

To open a program, simply move your cursor over the name of the program you want to open and click on it. This opens the program and brings up a new window on your screen that corresponds to the application you chose. You can also select the Create New Office Document selection from the Start Menu and then double-click on the type of document to open, which will also open the corresponding program.

To close any of the programs, you can simply click on the Close Button of the application's window, which is the small box with an "X" in it in the upper right-hand corner of the window. All Windows 95 programs have this Close Button , as well as a Minimize Button (small box with an underline in it) and a Resize

Button (small box with two overlapping windows in it), also in the upper right-hand corner of the screen.

As is common in today's modern computer programs, there are often many different ways to accomplish the same thing. You can close programs by several other methods as well. You can choose Exit from the pull-down File menu in the upper left-hand corner of the program's window, or right-click on the program's Button on the Taskbar and choose Close from the pop-up menu that appears. (Whenever a program is open in Windows 95, there will be a Button for it on the Taskbar.)

Creating a new document

There are also several ways to create new documents in Office. As with most Windows 9X applications, you can create a new document from within an open program by selecting the File pull-down menu and clicking on New.

Another way to do this would be to select the New Document Button from the main toolbar in either Word, Excel, or PowerPoint, which is the upper left-most Button that has a picture of a blank page in it.

Yet another way to create a new document is to click on the Start Button on the Taskbar, which brings up the Start Menu. Then move your mouse up and click on New Office Document in this pop-up menu. This opens a dialog box that allows you to choose which type of document you would like to create a Word document, an Excel spreadsheet, or a PowerPoint presentation.

The Save As option allows you to specify the name and location again, while leaving the original document unchanged.

Opening, closing, and saving existing files

The easiest way to open, close, and save files from any of the Office applications is from the File pull-down menu. Word, Excel, and PowerPoint all have the choices of Open, Close, Save, and Save As in their File menu. Simply select the File pull-down menu, then choose the option that corresponds to the action you want to do.

If you select Save, and are saving the document for the first time, you will get a dialog box that prompts you to name the document and tell the computer where to save the document. If you have previously saved the document or specified this information, clicking on Save automatically saves the current version of the document, with the existing name and location.

If you need to change either the name or location, or to save a new version of a document while still keeping the older version, use the Save As option, which allows you to specify the name and location again, while leaving the original document unchanged.

Getting online help

If you have a question or need help with a feature or command, a great resource is the extensive online help files that come with Office.

Simple explanations of the different Buttons on the various toolbars can be seen by moving your cursor over the Button -- However, not clicking on it-- and waiting a few seconds. A small box automatically pops up with a description of that Button. It disappears when you move the cursor somewhere else.

If you need help with a feature or command, access the extensive online help files that come with Office.

To get a more detailed explanation of a Button or some other area on the screen, go to the Help pull-down menu and select What is This (or press Shift + F1). Your cursor will change into an arrow with a question mark. Now whatever you click on brings up a detailed description of the area your cursor is on. If you click on text in a Word document, you will see information about the formatting, font, and style of the text. To turn the help cursor back to the regular cursor, press the Escape (Esc) key.

To access the online manuals, use the Help pull-down menu from any of the Office applications. From the Help menu, you can choose Contents and Index, which brings up a window with the table of contents and an index of the help manual for whatever application you are in when you go to Help. From these menus, you can double-click on topics to get to the manual pages that describe them. There is also a tab for a search command in the help files called Find.

There is also online help in the form of the animated Office Assistant, or "paper-clip guy" as he is sometimes called. This "assistant" comes up whenever you first launch your Office programs, and also whenever you click on the Office Assistant Button on the Stand port toolbar. This Button has a question mark on it and is supposed to give you information by letting you type in a question. It is only marginally helpful and can be very annoying.

Chapter 17

Word general

This section describes how to do the most common word processing tasks using Word. After reading this section, you should be able to enter and edit text into a document, cut-in addition;-paste, and change the fonts and character styles of your documents. We will also cover setting margins, using the spelling and grammar checkers, and printing documents.

To start a word processing session, you need to open Word and either create a new document or open an existing one. To create a new document, select the File pull-down menu and click on New. To open an existing document, select the File pull-down menu and click on Open, then select the document you want to open using the dialog box that appears.

Now you can enter text into your document by typing from the Keyboard. Your typing will be entered wherever the cursor is at the time you start typing. There are several Keyboard concepts to become familiar with when entering text into a Word document:

- Pressing Return moves the cursor to the next line.
- Pressing Delete or Backspace erases the character behind the cursor, or any text that is currently highlighted.
- You can highlight text by holding down the left Button on your mouse and dragging the mouse over the section of text you wish to highlight, then letting go of the mouse Button. The highlighted text will be replaced by whatever you type next.
- You can cut or copy sections of your Word document by highlighting the area of the document to be cut or copied, and selecting Cut or Copy from the Edit pull-down menu.
- You can paste sections (of text that you have previously cut or copied) into your Word document by placing the cursor at the point where you want to begin and selecting Paste from the Edit pull-down menu.

Once you have mastered these basic concepts, you will be on your way to creating documents of all kinds. The ability to cut-in addition;-paste is an incredibly powerful tool for creating and editing documents, and is probably the single largest advantage to writing on a computer using word processing software.

The ability to cut-in addition;-paste is probably the single largest advantage to writing on a computer using word processing software.

Fonts and **character styles**

Once you have some text in your document, you will probably want to make some adjustments to how it appears. There are many ways to change the appearance of your documents; However, the most common are to adjust the font and the character styles-- color, size, alignment, and so on.

To change any part of your existing document, select and highlight the section you wish to alter. Once the section is highlighted, any change you make in fonts or styles will affect the highlighted area.

Fonts are the different typefaces you use for the text in your document. You can choose different fonts for different parts of your document, and change the size and color of the type. Type can also be italicized, underlined, or set to bold face.

These type changes can be made from different Button s on the Formatting toolbar across the top of the window, or from the Font dialog box. If you are only going to change one aspect of the type, it is probably easier to use the Formatting toolbar; However, if you are making several changes, the Font dialog box is better.

On the Formatting toolbar, the Button with a bold B on it makes type boldface, the Button with an italicized I makes type italicized, and the Button with an underlined U is for underlining text. Clicking any of these Button s changes any highlighted text. If no text is highlighted, the change takes affect on text added after this Button is pressed.

One of the advantages of using the Font dialog box: If you do not know what font you want to use, it is easy to experiment and see how different fonts look.

There are also Button s on the Formatting toolbar for font, font size, style, alignment, and a few other options. You will recognize the Font Button because it has the name of the current font in it with a pull-down arrow to the right of the font name. Clicking and holding down on this Button brings up a list of available fonts. Drag your mouse down to another font name on this list to select a new font.

The Font Size Button is directly to the right of the Font Button, and has the current font size, in points, in it. This works just like the Font Button: By clicking and holding on the arrow at the right, you get a list of available font sizes. Move your mouse to one of the choices to change the font size.

You can also adjust all of these things from the Font dialog box, which you open by selecting Font from the Format pull-down menu. This brings up a dialog box with all the previously discussed choices, plus a Preview box to show what your choice will look like. This is one of the advantages of using the Font dialog box; if you do not know what font you want to use, it is easy to experiment and see how different fonts look. There is also a Button here to change the color of your text, and several Effects check-off boxes to further enhance your character style, such as subscript, embossing, and so on.

Margins, indenting, and **aligning**

A common need in word processing is to adjust the margins and alignment of a document. You can easily do this in Word, using the Formatting toolbar and the Page Setup and Paragraph dialog boxes.

To change the margins of a document, select the Page Setup from the File pull-down menu. This brings up the Page Setup dialog box, where you can change the margins, paper size, and layout of your document. New documents default to margins of 1 inch on top and bottom and 1.25 inches on left and right; if you want to change these, simply enter a new value into the corresponding field in the dialog box.

Like most operations in Word, highlighted text will be aligned when you click on one of the alignment Button s.

Margins are typically set the same for an entire document, or at least document sections. If you need to indent portions of text separately from the document margins, use the indent Button s or the Paragraph dialog box. The indent Button s are on the Formatting toolbar-- there is an Increase Indent Button with an arrow pointing towards the text and a Decrease Indent Button with an arrow pointing away. Clicking on either of these Button s changes the indentation of the paragraph your cursor is currently on by half an inch. You can also adjust the indentation indicators on the ruler at the top of the screen for a similar effect.

To bring up the Paragraph dialog box, select Paragraph from the Format pull-down menu. This brings up a dialog box that allows you to specify the indentations, spacing, line and page breaks, and alignment. Just like the Font dialog box, there is a Preview box that shows you what your choices will look like in your document.

Alignment refers to whether the lines of text are left justified, right justified, or centered. The alignment Button s are on the Formatting toolbar and in the Paragraph dialog box. The alignment Button s look like miniature text documents, with the lines either justified on the left, the right, or centered. Like most operations in Word, highlighted text will be aligned when you click on one of these Buttons.

Spelling, grammar, and **printing**

Word also includes a spelling checker and a grammar checker. The program checks everything you type in against its internal dictionary. If it sees a word it does not recognize, it underlines it with a red squiggly line. As with most things in Word, there are several different ways to deal with words that it thinks are misspelled.

If you only want to address a single word that Word thinks is misspelled, the easiest way to do this is to right-click on the word and choose either a corrected version of the word, Ignore, or Spelling from the pop-up menu.

Choosing Ignore tells Word that you want to leave the word as is, and choosing Spelling brings up the Spelling and Grammar dialog box.

You can also bring up the Spelling and Grammar dialog box by clicking on the Spelling and Grammar Button on the Stand port toolbar, which is the Button with "ABC" and a checkmark on it. This is probably the best way to deal with many misspellings or to check an entire document.

Be careful when using the Grammar checker: It will not always construct phrases that make sense!

From this dialog box, you see all the words that do not match spellings in the internal dictionary. You have the options Ignore and Ignore All, with Ignore telling Word to leave this one occurrence alone and Ignore All telling it to leave all occurrences of this spelling alone in this document.

You also have the option of Add, which adds the spelling of the specific word to the internal dictionary so that it will not be detected as a misspelling again. You will also be given a list of suggested corrections, from which you can select a replacement and then click Change to make the change.

If you have the Check Grammar box selected in the Spelling and Grammar dialog box, Word also makes suggestions for phrases it thinks are grammatically incorrect. You see the suggested change in this box. Again, choose the Change option to replace the phrase. Be careful when using the Grammar checker: It will not always construct phrases that make sense!

When you finally have a document you are ready to put down on paper, it is time to learn how to print from Word. This is as easy as clicking on the Print Button from the Stand port toolbar (the Button with a printer on it) or selecting Print from the File pull-down menu. In many cases you may want to first choose Print Preview by either pressing the Print Preview Button on the Stand port toolbar (the Button with a picture of a page of paper and a magnifying glass on it) or selecting Print Preview from the File pull-down menu. This gives a preview of how your text will fit onto the printed page and gives you an opportunity to make any changes before actually printing.

When you are ready to print the document and have either pressed the Print Button or selected Print from the File pull-down menu, you will get the Print dialog box. From this box, you specify how many copies to print, and which printer to use if your computer is connected to more than one printer on a network. You can also specify to only print certain pages of a document by filling in the Page Range box. Once these fields are specified-- the default is to print one copy of all the pages of the document-- simply click OK, and your document should be on its way to the printer.

Removing Office Specific HTML Tags From Pages You Saved As HTML

This is very easy. Just visit the Office Update site and download the Office HTML Filter. The Office HTML Filter is a tool you can use to remove Office-specific markup tags embedded in Office documents saved as HTML.

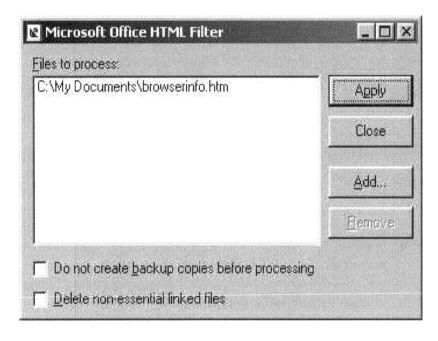

"This Application Requires Windows Installer" Error

If when you try and run Word. You get the message "The application requires Windows Installer." it tends to be for the following reason:

This error message is generated when you try to run the Office executables directly off the Setup CDs, and have not yet installed the programs.

Insert Office Setup CD1 into your CD-ROM drive, and run Setup.

To convert a PDF document from Adobe Acrobat Reader to Microsoft Word

 use one of the following methods appropriate for your version of Adobe Acrobat Reader.
To convert a PDF document from Adobe Acrobat Reader to Microsoft Word use one of the following methods appropriate for your version of Adobe Acrobat Reader.

Acrobat Reader.

Use the following steps to copy text from a PDF file if you are using Adobe Acrobat Reader:
1. Open your PDF document into Adobe Acrobat Reader.
2. Select the content of the current screen image that you want to use in Word by doing one of the following:
To select and copy text, do the following in Adobe Acrobat Reader:
a. On the Acrobat toolbar, click and hold the mouse on the Select Tool Button. This is the Button immediately to the right of the Zoom in Tool (Z) Button. Then click the Text Select Tool (V) toolbar Button.
b. Click and drag the I-beam mouse pointer over the text that you want to copy. The text will be selected (highlighted).
To select and copy a graphic, do the following:
a. On the Acrobat toolbar, click and hold the mouse on the Select Tool Button. This is the Button immediately to the right of the Zoom in Tool (Z) Button. Then click the Graphics Select Tool (V) toolbar Button.
b. Click and drag the cross-hair mouse pointer (the cross-hair mouse pointer is a large plus sign [+]) around the picture or graphic that you want to copy.
3. On the Edit menu, click Copy.
4. In Microsoft Word, click Paste on the Edit menu.

These 10 MS Word commands allow you to create documents quickly.

1. Restore a document in one-step with multiple levels of undo.

Word keeps track of your actions each time you make editing changes to your document. You can restore a document to all or part of its original state after making a series of editing changes all in one-step.

Click the pop-up menu on the Undo Button (located on the Stand port toolbar), then highlight all the actions you want to undo. When you click the last action in the list, you want undone, Word restores to document to the state it was prior to undoing the selected actions.

2. Use the Insert key to paste text from the clipboard.

Set up the Insert key so that it pastes text or graphics saved in the Clipboard into your document.

1. Choose Tools, Options.
2. Click the Edit tab.
3. Choose Use the INS key for paste.
4. Choose OK.
3. Right-click a word to find a synonym for it.

You can use the Thesaurus, or you can simply press Shift+F7 when the cursor is in a word. You can quickly select a synonym with these steps.

1. Right-click the word to open the shortcut menu.
2. Choose Synonyms at the bottom of the menu.
3. Click the synonym you want used in the cascading menu.
4. Change the case of selected text.

Word offers you a wide selection of change-case options. This makes it easy to change the capitalization of lots of text in one action.

1. Select all of the text in the paragraph or title to be changed.
2. Choose Format, Change Case (Alt+OE).
3. Select the appropriate radio Button.
- Choose Sentence case to capitalize only the first word and lowercase all others.
- Choose Lowercase to lowercase all letters.
- Choose Uppercase to uppercase all letters.
- Choose Title Case to capitalize the first letter of all the words in the text.
- Choose Toggle Case to capitalize all lowercase letters and lowercase all capital letters in the text.
5. Use the AutoCorrect feature to have Word automatically correct your misspellings.
1. Choose Tools, AutoCorrect.
2. With the AutoCorrect tab selected in the AutoCorrect dialog box, type a word you often misspell (such as perceive) in the Replace text box.
3. Type the word the way it is supposed to be spelled (perceive) in the With text box.
4. Choose Add, then repeat the steps or choose OK.

After adding a word in this manner to the AutoCorrect dialog box, Word will automatically correct that misspelling of it anytime you incorrectly enter it in any document.

6. Inserting text or graphics quickly as AutoText entries.

You can use the AutoText feature to insert stock phrases (Biloby, Biloby, Sax, and Tipton) or stock graphics (such as the company logo).

1. Select the text or graphic to be automatically entered.

2. Press Alt+F3 to open the Create AutoText entry.
3. Type the abbreviation (such as corplogo) you will use to insert the text or graphic (do not use spaces) and choose OK.

To insert the stock text or graphic in the document, type in its abbreviation, then press F3.

7. Using Document Map view to navigate a long document.

The Document Map feature makes it easy to move to a particular place in a long document that has been formatted with headings.

1. Choose View, then Document Map or click the Document Map Button on the Stand port toolbar to open the Document Map pane to the left.
2. The Document Map pane shows all the headings that you have entered in the document. To move the cursor directly to that place in the document, click the heading in the Document Map pane.
3. To compress the list of headings, right-click somewhere in the Document Map pane, then select highest level of the heading that you want shown in the pop-up menu.

After moving the cursor to the desired heading in the document, click the Document Map Button to close its pane and begin editing.

8. Use the Format Painter to format document text on the fly.

You can use the Format Painter Button to copy the formatting from any paragraph or heading to the rest of the document.

1. Format the paragraph text or heading as needed.
2. Click the cursor somewhere in the formatted text.
3. Double-click the Format Painter Button on the Format toolbar.
4. Drag the Format Painter cursor through the paragraph or title you want formatted in the same manner.

5. Paint all the paragraphs or heading text that you want formatted with the Format Painter Button.
6. When you have finished painting, click the Format Painter Button to turn this feature off.
9. Insert AutoText into document headers and footers.

In Word 2000, you can create headers and footers that use stock text (such as page numbers, author's name, filename, created on date, or the date last printed) in a flash by using the Insert AutoText feature.

1. Choose View, then Header and Footer to open Header area and display the Header and Footer toolbar.
2. Position the cursor at the place in the header where you want the stock text inserted.
3. Click the pop-up arrow on the Insert AutoText Button, and then select the type of text to insert (such as page for page number).
4. Press the down arrow if you want to insert text in the document header.
5. Repeat step three.
6. Choose the close Button when you have finished adding text to the document header in addition;/or footer.
10. Email current document.

You can email a copy of the current document you are editing without having to open your email program.

1. Click the Email Button on the Stand port toolbar.
2. Enter the recipient's email address in the To text box (or click the To Button and select the address from you address book).
3. Click the Send a Copy Button.

Chapter 18

Excel general

This section describes how to do the most common spreadsheet tasks using Excel. After reading this section, you should be able to create a worksheet, enter and edit data, cut-in addition;-paste data, and move and delete data in your worksheets. We will also cover formulas and functions, formatting, customizing, and printing worksheets.

To clarify the terminology used here: Excel is generally thought of as a "spreadsheet" program. A spreadsheet is a matrix of rows and columns of data that can be manipulated using mathematical calculations in different ways, such as keeping running totals. Excel calls its spreadsheet files "worksheets" and keeps them together in "workbooks". A workbook is just a collection of worksheets.

To start an Excel session, open Excel and either create a new worksheet or open an existing one. To create a new worksheet, click on the New Button on the Stand port toolbar. To open an existing worksheet, click on the Open Button on the Stand port toolbar or select the File pull-down menu, then click on Open and use the dialog box that shows up to select the worksheet to open.

Excel calls its spreadsheet files worksheets. A workbook is a collection of worksheets.

You can also create a new worksheet based on one of the included templates in Excel. To do this, select New from the File pull-down menu, then select the Spreadsheet Solutions tab to get access to the templates. Now you can click on any of the provided templates to see an example of it in the Preview box. To open a worksheet with a chosen template, just double-click the template. You will probably notice some similarities to the Word interface. There is a

Stand port toolbar and a Formatting toolbar, with many of the same options that Word has. You can Cut, Copy, and Paste, and Print and Print Preview from the Stand port toolbar, and you can adjust the font, size, and style of your type from the Formatting toolbar.

Now you can enter data into your worksheet by typing from the Keyboard. Your typing appears wherever the cursor is at the time you start typing. There are several important concepts to become familiar with when entering data into an Excel document:

• The rectangle that corresponds to one row heading and one column heading is called the "active cell." A cell can hold one item of data, which can be a number, a formula, or text. The active cell is where you type in data.
• The rows are labeled numerically starting at 1, and the columns are labeled alphabetically starting at A. A cell is identified by its column label and row label; for example, "1A".
• Pressing Return moves the active cell down one row.
• Pressing Tab moves the active cell one cell to the right.
• Pressing the arrow keys moves the active cell in the direction of the arrow key.
• Typing a cell location, like 1A, in the Name box on the toolbar moves the active cell to that location.
• Pressing Delete (or Backspace) erases the data in the active cell, or any group of cells currently highlighted.
• You can highlight data cells by holding down the left Button on your mouse and dragging the mouse over the section of the worksheet you wish to highlight, then letting go of the mouse Button.
• You can cut or copy sections of your Excel worksheet by highlighting the area to be cut or copied and selecting Cut or Copy from the Edit pull-down menu.
• You can paste sections (that you have previously cut or copied) into your Excel worksheet by placing the cursor at the point where the added section should begin and selecting Paste from the Edit pull-down menu.

- **Formulas and functions**

The powers of spreadsheet programs like Excel lie in their ability to use formulas that perform mathematical calculations on groups of data. You can set up a formula based on a specific group of cells, and if the data in the cells changes, the program automatically updates the outcome of the formula. Imagine a spreadsheet like a checkbook-balancing program-- when you enter in the amount of the check you just wrote, it automatically adjusts your balance to reflect the latest subtraction.

There are many formulas you can use in an Excel worksheet; However, the most common ones are very familiar if you have ever taken a mathematics course. Most formulas are constructed of cell labels (A1, B2, etc.) and mathematical operators (+, -, *, /, etc.).

You can set up a formula based on a specific group of cells, and if the data in the cells changes, Excel automatically updates the outcome of the formula.

To enter a formula directly into the active cell, start by typing "=". This equal sign tells Excel that what you enter next is a formula, not plain old text. A typical formula might look something like "=A1+B1+C1," which would give the sum of the three values in A1, B1, and C1.

You can enter a formula into a worksheet in several ways:

- You can enter it directly into the active cell, making sure to begin with an "=".
- You can highlight the cell you want to put the formula in, then go to the Formula Bar at the top of the worksheet and enter the formula there.
- You can click on the Edit Formula Button, which is the Button with the "=" on it next to the Formula Bar, and enter it from the Edit Formula dialog box.

• You can specify which cells to use in a formula by typing them right into the formula. You can also click on the appropriate cells when the formula is expecting a cell label and it will put the cell(s) you click on into the formula.

Functions are the predefined formulas that come with Excel. The most common function is AutoSum; it is so common, in fact, that it has its own Button on the Stand port toolbar. You can use AutoSum to total up rows or columns of data.

To see all of the available functions, bring up the Paste Function dialog box. To do this, select Function from the Insert pull-down menu or press the Paste Function Button on the Stand port toolbar.

You can type the function name directly into an active cell, making sure to start with an "=," or you can also type the function into the Formula bar of the active cell.

The most common function is AutoSum; it is so common, in fact, that it has its own Button on the Stand port toolbar.

When you are looking at the Paste Function dialog box, you will see a list of function categories on the left and a list of corresponding functions on the right. Each category choice has a different set of functions, and when you single-click on a function name, a description of the function appears at the bottom of the dialog box. You can also click on the Help Button in this dialog box to get a more detailed description with syntax examples.

Two other ways of specifying which data cells the function or formula should be applied to be by indicating a range of cells and by assigning names to ranges of cells. You can specify a range of cells, like A1+B1+C1+D1+E1, as A1:E1. You can assign names to ranges of cells in the Define Name dialog box, which you access from the Insert pull-down menu. Then you can use the name in the formula or function, such as =SUM (sales).

Formatting, customizing, and printing

There are many options for formatting your data, from the stand port text-formatting options we saw in Word to some specialized numerical formats unique to Excel. There is a Formatting toolbar, with the same Button s for boldface, italics, and underlining text, and aligning text right justified, left justified, or centered. And there are Button s on this toolbar for Currency style ($), Percentage style (%), Comma style (,), and an Increase Decimal Place Button and a Decrease Decimal Place Button (these Button s have ".0" with arrows pointing left or right).

Print Preview shows how your data will fit onto the printed worksheet and gives you an opportunity to make changes before printing.

It is also easy to change the width of your columns and height of your rows, and align text and numbers. To change the size of a column or row, just move your mouse to the space between two column letters or row numbers; the cursor will turn into a cross. Now you can click and drag the border of the cell to wherever you want it. There are also alignment Button s on the Formatting toolbar, where you can specify a given range of cells to be right-, left-, or center-justified.

When you are finally ready to print your worksheet, you can select the Print Button from the Stand port toolbar (the Button with a printer on it) or selecting Print from the File pull-down menu. If you want to see what your worksheet will look like on paper, choose Print Preview by either pressing the Print Preview Button on the Stand port toolbar (it has a picture of a page of paper and a magnifying glass on it) or selecting Print Preview from the File pull-down menu. This shows how your data will fit onto the printed worksheet and gives you an opportunity to make any changes before actually printing.

To print the worksheet, press the Print Button, or select Print from the File pull-down menu, you will get the Print dialog box. From this box, you can specify how many copies to print, and which printer to use if your computer is connected to more than one printer on a network. You can also specify to only print certain pages of a worksheet by filling in the Print Range box.

Once these fields are specified (the default prints one copy of all the pages of the worksheet), just click OK, and your worksheet should be on its way to the printer.

Chapter 19

PowerPoint general

This section describes how to do the most common presentation tasks using PowerPoint. After reading this section, you should be able to create a presentation, use the AutoContent wizard, and work with presentation slides. We will also cover adding clip art to your slides and previewing and printing presentations.

PowerPoint presentations are groups of slides that you create, mixing text, and graphics. These slides can be viewed on computers, projection screens, and printed on transparencies. PowerPoint has many built-in styles, some of which you will recognize if you have sat in on any sales meetings lately.

To start a PowerPoint session, open PowerPoint and either create a new presentation or open an existing one. When you launch the program, you can choose from three ways to create or open a presentation: AutoContent Wizard, Templates, or do it yourself. You can also select New from the File pull-down menu to create a presentation.

The AutoContent Wizard asks you questions about your presentation and suggests formats based on many predefined presentation types. It includes strategies for topics to cover that are specific to the type of presentation you have chosen, with choices ranging from Marketing Plan to Presenting a Technical Report.

If you choose Templates, you are taken right to the New Presentation dialog box, where the predefined templates are. Single clicking any of the templates brings up an example in the Preview box, and double-clicking on one starts a presentation in that template. You will then be shown the New Slide dialog box, where you can choose the layout of the slide.

Choosing "Create a new Presentation" using a blank page bypasses the templates and takes you directly to the New Slide dialog box.

When you click OK on your selected layout, you will see a screen with an image of the slide on it, along with text, image, and chart areas, depending on the given layout. Click on a text area to type your text into it. Double-click on an image area to get the Microsoft Clip Gallery, from which you can choose and insert an image, or import an image from somewhere else. Double-click on a chart area to bring up a Microsoft Graph window that allows you to enter data and represent it as a graph.

When entering text, you have many of the same editing options we have seen in the other Office applications.

When entering text into a text area, you have many of the same editing options we have seen in the other Office applications. There is a Formatting toolbar, with the familiar options for boldface, italics, and underlined, plus a new Button for shadowed.

Previewing and **printing**

There are several ways to view and edit the slides in your presentation. The View pull-down menu offers choices for Slide, Outline, Slide Sorter, and Slide Show, among others. The Slide view gives you a full-screen view of the first slide; you can use the scroll bar to page through all of the slides. The Outline view gives you a list of the slides, with small icons and names. You can click on the slide icon to bring up the full-screen image of any slide. The Slide Sorter view gives larger versions of the slides, along with their sequence numbers.

From either the Outline or Slide Sorter view, you can drag slides around and change the order of your presentation. There are also very small Button s for each of these views in the lower left-hand corner of the screen. You can edit any slide when it is in the full-screen view.

The Slide Show view gives you just that-- a slide show of your presentation.

The Slide Show view gives you just that-- a slide show of your presentation. You can click anywhere on a slide to advance to the next slide, or press N. Alternatively, you can automate the slides by right-clicking on a slide in the Slide Sorter view and selecting Slide Transition. From the Slide Transition dialog box, you can set the time between slides and the effects to be used during the transitions.

You can print your slides on transparencies for an overhead projector or create paper handouts of your presentation. Select Print from the File pull-down menu and you get the Print hand out dialog box. You have the usual print options, plus a choice of how many slides to print on each page. To print transparencies, select one per page, and choose the correct size in the Page Setup dialog box (also under the File pull-down menu).

Chapter 20

Outlook general

This section describes how to do the most common email and information management tasks using Microsoft Outlook. After reading this section, you should be able to send and receive email messages. You will learn how to organize and store these messages and use the Address Book. We will also cover the use of the Scheduler and Contact list that are part of Outlook.

Outlook is a combination personal organizer and email program. It opens up in your Inbox, However, has a list of other functions that you can scroll through, including Calendar and Contacts. You can check your email from the Inbox and access other email options by clicking on the Mail Button on the Outlook bar.

Email

The Inbox is where you read your new email messages. You can select Check for New Mail from the Tools pull-down menu to check your mail account at any time, as long as you are connected to the Internet. They are listed in the order received. Just double-click on the message in the Inbox; this brings up the entire message.

The Inbox is where you read your new email messages.

When you view an email message, you have the choice of saving the message, moving it to a folder, or deleting it (all from the File pull-down menu and Button s on the toolbar). You can also reply to the sender of a message and Forward the message to other people.

To send an email message, click the New Mail Message Button on the toolbar or select New Mail message from the File pull-down menu. This brings up the Message dialog box. From this box, enter the address of the recipient(s) and the text of your message.

To include an attached file along with a message you are sending, click on the Insert File Button (which looks like a paper clip) or select File from the Insert pull-down menu. This brings up the Insert File dialog box, which allows you to browse or search through your system to find the file you want to attach.

Sorting and **the Address Book**

To keep your messages organized, you can create different folders set up to save email on related topics. Then after you read an incoming message you want to keep, you can move it to the appropriate folder. Select the Move to Folder Button either the Move to Folder Button either the Move to Folder Button either the Move to Folder Button either the Move to Folder Button either on the toolbar or the Move to Folder selection from the Edit pull-down menu, and then use the Move Items dialog box to either pick the folder to use or create a new one.

To keep track of people you regularly send email to Outlook has an Address Book. You can open the Address Book dialog box by selecting Address Book from the Tools pull-down menu or clicking on the Button that looks like a book. Select the New Entry choice from the File pull-down menu to enter a new address. Clicking on the To: field Button in a Message dialog box brings up the Select Names screen, which contains the information in your address book.

From this point, you can select a recipient from your Address Book by double-clicking on the address. This gives you the ability to write and send messages to your friends without having to remember their email addresses.

Scheduler and **Contact List**

Outlook also lets you schedule meetings and appointments in a Calendar and maintain a Contact List, as well as a few other information management features.

You can enter notations into any time period of any day on your calendar.

To work on the Calendar, select the Calendar menu from the Outlook menu bar; for the Contact List, select Contacts.

When the Calendar menu is in effect, you will see both a daily and monthly display. You can enter notations into any time period of any day on your calendar. Clicking on a day in the monthly display brings up that day and allows you to enter in-- or edit existing-- scheduling information.

To schedule an appointment, bring up the Appointment dialog box by either clicking on the New Appointment Button or selecting New Appointment from the Calendar pull-down menu. Here you can specify a subject and location, and schedule a reminder to be delivered to your PC at some predetermined time.

The Contact list is maintained by entering information into the Contact dialog box, accessed by either clicking on the New Contact Button or selecting New Contact from the Contacts pull-down menu. Here you will find a wide array of information fields to fill in for each contact. Contacts can be grouped together by company. You can also send email messages and schedule meetings directly with people on your Contact List by choosing either New Message for Contact or New Meeting for Contact from the Contacts pull-down menu.

Resources

Well, there is your introduction to the brave new world of Office. Virtually anything you need to do can be accomplished with this little suite of tools and tricks-- word processing via Word; household budgeting and simple accounting with Excel; organizing your life with Outlook; and spiffing up your presentations with a little help from PowerPoint.

Get Some Assistance

The most pervasive (some would say annoying) feature of Office is the Office Assistant. Do you value the help the animated paper clip provides However, cannot stand the clip itself? Right-click the little bugger for options on what to do with it. The Choose Assistant option lets you pick another helper. If all that jumping around drives you batty try the Office logo, the calmest of the Assistants. The Animate option makes the existing Assistant move around a little (for those short on entertainment). Under Options, you can select what kind of help the Assistant will give you (such as displaying only high-priority tips or showing programming hints).

However, the two most useful options are See Tips, which can provide a variety of hints and shortcuts, and Hide Assistant, which puts the helper away. Bring the Assistant back when you need help by pressing the F1 key or clicking on the question mark in the word balloon on the toolbar.

If the Assistant rankles you so much that you do not mind throwing out the baby with the bathwater, you can make it go away for good:

1. Right-click the animated Assistant, and choose Options.
2. Select the Options tab, and uncheck the Respond to F1 key.
3. Exit Office.
4. Restart Office, and the Assistant will be gone.

When you need help in the future, press the F1 key to bring up a stand port Windows Help index. However, consider carefully before taking the drastic measure of eliminating the Assistant. The Help index makes you hunt for answers; the Assistant brings them to you.

Format Painting

Want to quickly apply the format of a section of your document to another section? Just use your mouse to highlight the section (a headline, a paragraph, or a word) that has the desired format. Click the Format Painter icon on the stand port toolbar, and use your mouse to highlight the section you want to format. The selection is instantly reformatted.

This easy, timesaving solution is a good way to make sure formatting is consistent when you are expanding a document that was created using a heavily formatted template. You can also use this method when you are adding to a document someone else created.

By default, Word corrects your spelling and grammar as you go. If you find this irritating and would rather have the program check only when you request it to do so, select Tools/Options/Spelling & Grammar from the menu bar, and click to remove the check marks from the "Check spelling as you type" and "Check grammar as you type" boxes.

Travel Fast Around Documents

Instead of scrolling down every page and scanning each paragraph to move around in your Word documents, travel fast using the Select Browse Object Button. When you click this Button (located in the bottom right corner of your screen between the two sets of double arrows), you get a pop-up Button menu with the following options. Go To, Find, Browse By Edits, Browse By Heading,

Browse By Graphics, Browse By Table, Browse By Field, Browse By Endnote, Browse By Footnote, Browse By Comment, Browse By Section, or Browse By Page. Select one of the Button s to change the function of the double arrow Button s on either side of the Select Browse Object Button. For example, if you click the Browse By Table option, you can then go to the previous table in your document by clicking the double up-arrow Button. Similarly, clicking the double down-arrow Button will take you to the next table.

Add Reminders

ToolTips are those little bits of text that pop up when you point the mouse at a Button or menu item inside many Windows 9X programs. They take the worry out of remembering all of Access's arcane controls. Now you can attach these helpful items to fields, Button s, or other items on your forms:

1. Open the form in Design View, then right-click the item you want to work with.
2. From the pop-up menu, select Properties to open the dialog box.
3. Click the Other tab in the dialog box, and then type your ToolTip text in the Control Tip Text area.
4. When you are done, close the Properties dialog box, and save your form.

Recycle Your Letters

Most people do not reinvent the wheel with each piece of business correspondence. If you want to reuse the format in addition;/or text of an existing letter, Word Letter Wizard makes it easy. Open the document you want to emulate, and then select Tools/Letter Wizard from the menu bar. When applied to an existing letter, the Letter Wizard "reads" the document and displays a tabbed dialog box that lets you change only the key parts of the letter (such as the sender and recipient info). You are not forced through every step of the Wizard.

Add Cool Background Music

PowerPoint's Clip Gallery Live has some basic musical backgrounds, However, funkier selections are available in the Custom Soundtracks Editor (found in the Value Pack folder of the Office CD-ROM).

Once you have installed the Editor, choose Custom Soundtrack from the Slide Show menu. You can select from a wide variety of styles and motifs to help set the mood and reinforce your message.

 do not forget that you can also add stand port WAV files to your presentation or even play a track from an audio CD by choosing Movies and Sounds from the Insert menu.

Turn Presentations into Websites

You can turn any PowerPoint presentation into a series of Web pages by using the File menu's Save As HTML option. This brings up the Save As HTML Wizard to lead you step-by-step through the process. The Wizard is full of useful Web-oriented tools. You can, for example, select a normal layout or use browser frames, choose a graphics type, pick your resolution, add navigation Button s, and even add a link that lets users download the latest version of Internet Explorer.

Turn Presentations into Websites

You can turn any PowerPoint presentation into a series of Web pages by using the File menu's Save As HTML option. This brings up the Save As HTML Wizard to lead you step-by-step through the process. The Wizard is full of useful Web-oriented tools. You can, for example, select a normal layout or use browser frames,

choose a graphics type, pick your resolution, add navigation
Button s, and even add a link that lets users download the latest
version of Internet Explorer.

Add Narration To PowerPoint

With PowerPoint, you can easily add voice narration to your
presentation. (You will need a sound card and microphone, of
course.) A recorded narration integrated with your presentation
makes it easy for you to distribute your presentation and your
presentation and is a perfect way to get info to people who cannot
make it to a live version. You can even record your presentation as
you deliver it. Here is how:

1. Open your presentation.
2. From the Slide Show menu, choose Record Narration.
3. When you are ready to proceed, click OK, and start your
narration.

PowerPoint will attach your recorded comments to the presentation
and will automatically change slides at the correct points when you
run the presentation later. You can choose several sound-quality
levels; the default Radio Quality is sufficient for voice-overs and
uses about 10K for each second of narration. A five-minute speech
consumes some 300K.

Create A Splash Screen

In the world of commercial software, splash screens are the
graphics that appear while the program is busy trying to pull its act
together and start running. Now you can add the same professional
touch to your databases:

1. Create an image with the Paint applet built into Windows or
with your favorite graphics program. You can even grab images
from CD-ROMs or Web-based clip art libraries. (Remember to

observe copyright laws, though--you do not want to tangle with a bunch of lawyers by illegally using someone else's artwork.)

2.   Save the picture as a Windows bitmap, file (BMP). Name the image file to match your database (for example, if your database is named medicine, your splash screen file should be called medicine.bmp). Be sure to save the image in the same folder as your database.

The next time anyone opens the database, the splash screen will hop into action first.

Find Chart Tips

Beneath any element of an Excel chart, there is a wealth of information. To access it, simply move your mouse cursor over the data point you are interested in. Chart Tips pop up automatically to identify the different components of the chart.

Conditional Formatting

Color-coding your data lets you tell at a glance whether your numbers are up or down. Using Excel's conditional formatting features, you can set up your sheet so that cells change colors depending on what their values are--a great way to make your cells easy to read:

1.   Select the cells that you want to color-code. To select noncontiguous cells, hold down Ctrl as you click.

2.   Select Format/Conditional Formatting. In the Conditional Formatting dialog box, you will set the conditions for the cells. In the first field on the left, decide whether you want the condition based on the value of a cell or formula. In the second field, select which conditional terms apply. In the third field, fill in the value for the cell, or use the third and fourth to fill in a range. For example, if you wanted to create a conditional format for a Total

cell, you could select Cell Value Is for the first field, "Greater than or equal to" for the second, and enter 1,000 in the third field as the value.

3.   In the same dialog box, click Format to set the cell's appearance when the condition is met. You can set options related to font, border, and pattern. If you just want to set the color, choose the Patterns tab, and select a color for the cell. For our example, you might select green, so that the Total cell will glow green when it hits the 1,000 mark.

4.   Click OK to complete the first condition.

5.   If you want to add another condition to the cell, click Add and repeat the steps to fill in Condition 2. Otherwise, click OK to put the conditional format in place.

Delay Message Delivery

Just because you do not want to send a particular message today, does not mean you cannot go ahead and write it. If you use Outlook's Delay Delivery feature, you can write your messages while you are thinking about them, and then send them on a future date.

Create the message you want to send in the future, and then click the Options tab. Click the "Do not deliver before" check box, and fill in the desired delivery date. When you click Send, the message will be held in your Outbox until the specified date, and then delivered to all the recipients.

Auto Text Buttons

Word lets you assign common phrases, such as "To Whom It May Concern:" or "Yours truly" to Button s on your toolbar. If you commonly type one of these phrases over and over, this feature can be really handy If you would like to assign a few phrases to Button s in your Word toolbar, choose Tools/Customize and then click on the Command stab. In the list box, locate and click on AutoText. Locate the phrase you are interested in assigning to a Button, and use the mouse to drag it to a toolbar.

With the Button on the toolbar, you can add the phrase to a document by simply clicking on the Button.

Replace And Count

Here is a little Word trick you might find useful. If your document consists of a bunch of different topic headings that all have the same style, you can count the number of topics in a document by simply counting the occurrences of the style, provided that style is not used for anything else.

Choose Edit/Replace. When the Replace dialog box opens, click on More. Now click in the Find What text entry box and then click on Format/Style. Choose the style you want to count.

Next, click in the Replace With text entry box, click on Format, and repeat the above procedure. Click on Replace All and Word will replace the style with itself leaving the document intact. After making all the replacements, Word will report the number of replacements made. This number represents the number of occurrences of that style in the document. Click on Close to do away with the dialog box.

Special Find And Replace

You know how to use Find and Replace to locate and change words in Microsoft Word. We have even discussed using Find and Replace to replace styles. If you take a close look at the Find and Replace dialog box, you will see that you can also use it to locate and change other document features.

Let us take a look. Run Word and load a document. Press Ctrl-H to open the Find and Replace dialog box. Now click on the More Buttons to get to the expanded feature list and click on Format. As you can see from the menu, you can find and replace fonts, paragraphs, tabs, languages, frames, styles, and highlights.

This offers some possibilities for those documents under development. For example, you could highlight a sentence or paragraph that is not thoroughly researched. The highlighting will remind you to do the research; and if you need to make changes later, you can use Find and Replace to locate (and perhaps make changes) to the highlighted text. When finished, all you have to do is remove the highlighting.

Create Instant Tables

If you are in a hurry or do not have time to learn the ins and outs of database design, you can get your information slotted into a basic table very quickly. Click the Tables tab in the Database dialog box, and click New. Then select the Datasheet View in the New Table dialog box, and click OK. A blank table is automatically created, ready for your information.

Add Shadows To Text

Want to use shadowed and other special fonts in Word. Here is what you do: Choose Format/Font, then click the Font tab. To produce shadowed characters in your selected font, select the Shadow check box, and then click OK. While you are at it, you might want to try some of the other special effects.

Special WordArt Effect

You know that WordArt allows a large number of special effects. However, along with the special effects that you can see, there are others that aren't quite as obvious. For example, if you change the width of your text's borderlines, you can create a completely new effect.

To check this out, insert some WordArt into a Word document by choosing Insert, Picture, and WordArt. After you size and place your new WordArt, click on it and then click on the Format WordArt Button in the WordArt floating toolbar (it looks like a bucket pouring paint). When the Format WordArt dialog box opens, click on the Colors and Lines tab.

Not all the WordArt selections have lines. If you happened to choose one of these, just click on OK to close the dialog box and go back to the beginning to select a WordArt style that has lines.

When your sample WordArt uses lines, you will see line color, style, and weight listed. Increase the weight. Try something rather heavy, perhaps 2 or 3 points. Click on OK.

After you see how the new border looks, you might want to try a new line color. Select the WordArt and click on Format WordArt again. This time select a new line color and click on OK.

This is one you can experiment with. Sometimes a combination of color and line widths can produce some very striking effects. do not hesitate to try some very wide line widths. We have seen some very good effects produced by using as much as 4.0 point lines.

Counting The Days

If you would like to know how many days left until Christmas, run Excel and type ="12/25/97"-"11/01/97" (or whatever the current date is) into a cell. Excel will return the number of days (54) between the two dates. The trick here is to remember the quotes. If you do not use quotes, you will get some very strange results.

Getting Converted

Since much of the world expresses its temperatures in centigrade (or Celsius) and we in the USA most often use Fahrenheit, having a way to quickly switch between the two can be helpful. Excel comes to the rescue with a command named CONVERT. To see how it works, type 68 into cell A1. Now move to cell A3 and type in =CONVERT(A1, "F", "C") and press Enter. This formula converts Fahrenheit (F) to Centigrade (C) and the result should be 20. If you need to convert from Centigrade to Fahrenheit, type in =CONVERT (A1, "C", "F") and press Enter. If you left 68 in A1, the new result should be 154.4. Note: if the Convert function does not work for you, choose Tools|Add-Ins. Make sure the Analysis Tool Pak option is turned on and click on OK.

Open Everything At Once

Like many other programs, Office applications let you open more than one file at once. In the File Open dialog box, hold down the Ctrl key while selecting as many files as you like. Click OK, and they will all open.

Tracking Recent Files

Office takes the stand port Recently Opened Files list to its next logical step for an office suite. Right-click the toolbar in any Office app; select the Web toolbar. Click the down arrow next to the name of the current document, and pick any document from the list. Office will open the file in its native application. Office even knows to open your browser to return you to recently visited Web sites.

Multilingual Spell-Check

If your documents include non-English text, your stand port spelling checker will not be much help when you try to inspect those sections. Luckily, Word allows you to designate selections of text to be checked by different dictionaries. For example, you may have included a quote from a French philosopher. To make sure that it will be spell-checked using a French dictionary, select the text and choose Tools/Language/Set Language. Pick the appropriate language from the list, and click OK. When you spell-check your entire document, you will be running a smarter, more effective, multilingual check. (To take advantage of this feature, you do have to have the appropriate supplemental dictionaries installed. If you have problems, try-reinstalling Word with all the dictionaries you plan to use selected.)

Adding A Watermark

A *watermark* is a faint background image that shows up behind the text or other images in your document. You can watermark your documents with your name, company logo, product-specific brand, or some other icon:

1. Select View/Header And Footer to open the Header And Footer toolbar.
2. Click the Show/Hide Document Text Button on the Header And Footer toolbar. (This step is not mandatory, However, seeing the full page, without the document's text, may be useful.)
3. Select Insert/Picture to get a selection of graphics choices. Office provides some clip art and word art options, or you can insert an image that you have created or saved in your own files.
4. Once you have selected the image you want to insert and clicked OK, use your mouse to drag the image to the place you want it to appear on the page. Remember, the image will fade into the background once you exit the Header And Footer screen, so do not worry if it appears too bright or bold.
5. Click Close on the Header And Footer toolbar. Your document now has a watermark that will appear on every page.

If you want to edit or move the watermark, select View/Header And Footer to redisplay the Header And Footer screen, and make your changes.

If you use clip art or import an image, you may find that wherever the image extends into the document, the document text wraps around it rather than overlaps it. To correct this, display the Header And Footer screen, right-click the image, and select the Format item option from the menu. From the dialog box that opens, choose the Wrapping tab, and select None from the top row, then click OK. The image should now appear under the text instead.

Scattering Of Logos

If you have special logos that you use frequently in your Word documents, you can use AutoText to make inserting them quick and easy.

To store a logo in AutoText, open a Word document and choose Insert, Picture, and From File. Choose the file you want to use as a logo. Once the picture is in the Word document, size it. Now right-click the logo and choose Format Picture. Click the Wrapping tab and then click Tight and Both Sides. Click OK.

Next, choose Insert, AutoText, and New. Type in MyLogo and click OK. Now your new logo (and its formatting) is stored in AutoText. To insert the logo, place the cursor where you want to insert the logo. Choose Insert, AutoText, Normal, MyLogo, and the logo will appear in the text. Use the mouse to drag it into the correct position.

Save Keystrokes

Do not let bulleted or numbered lists slow you down--let Word make them for you. To start a bulleted list, just type *, a space, and your sentence. When you press Enter, Word automatically replaces the asterisk with a bullet, indents the information, and places a bullet on the next line. When you are done with the bulleted list, just press Enter twice, and Word will end the list and return the cursor to the left margin.

This same technique works for numbered lists, too. Type 1, a space, and a sentence. When you press Enter, the indention will be adjusted, and the new line will be ready with the next number. As with bulleted lists, pressing Enter twice ends the list and returns the spacing to normal.

Review Everyone's Changes

Word 6.0 contained a nifty feature called Revisions that let you track changes made by various people in a collaborative project. Revisions made by different people showed up in different colors. Word has renamed and improved this feature. Now called Track Changes, it lets you see who made each change simply by holding the cursor over the edited text--a text box containing the editor's name pops up.

To track everyone's changes, select Tools/Track Changes/Highlight Changes from the menu bar, and check all the boxes in the Highlight Changes dialog box. To review a document's changes, right-click any toolbar, select the Reviewing toolbar from the shortcut menu, and click the Next Change icon.

Save Your Presentation In Older Formats

If you need to share your presentations with people who have older versions of PowerPoint, just use the expanded PowerPoint translators. With your PowerPoint presentation onscreen, choose Save As from the File menu. In the Save As Type box, choose your format. Choices include PowerPoint 95, PowerPoint 4, and PowerPoint 3, among others.

Create Speaker Notes

PowerPoint lets you create speaker notes while you design the content of a slide. With a slide onscreen, select View/Speaker Notes from the main menu. Type your notes next to the appropriate slide number, then drag the Notes box off to the side of the screen so you can work on your main slide.

Put Art In Your Charts

Want to add an impressive background to an Excel bar or line chart? The option exists, and the effects can be stunning:

1. Right-click the plot area (the part behind the data points), and select Format Plot Area.
2. Under the Patterns tab, click the Fill Effects Button, and experiment with the options under the Gradient, Texture, and Patterns tabs. You can even import a photograph or other graphic under the Picture tab.
3. Once you have gotten the desired effect, click OK twice.

Lay Out Text Smoothly

Use the Merge Cells tool in Excel to smoothly display blocks of text in a spreadsheet:

1. Select the group of cells where you want the text to appear, and right-click to bring up the shortcut menu.

2. Choose Format Cells.

3. Select the Alignment tab, and click the Wrap Text and Merge Cells options. Now the text will smoothly fill the merged cells without spilling over into adjacent cells.

Turn Databases Into Websites

Access's new Publish to the Web Wizard   lets you quickly create Web pages from tables, reports, and forms in your database. And if you use Microsoft's Internet Information Server on your network, you can even create Web pages that update themselves every time someone checks them out. For all the details, click the Office Assistant, and search for publishing to HTML.

Customize Outlook

To customize Outlook's basic functionality, begin by exploring the Options dialog box, using the What Is feature to find out what each item does before you start tinkering. Simply select Tools/Options from the menu bar, and right-click various items to pull up additional information.

Keeping Your Old Office

If you would like to install Microsoft Office and still retain (for a while anyway) your old Office 4.x or Office 95, all your have to do is tell Office Setup not to delete your old version (you will be asked--just watch for the message).

Because Office will be placed into the Registry, double- clicking a document icon will open the appropriate Office application. However, you can still open an older (Office 4.x or Office 95) application and then open documents by choosing File|Open.

Note, too, that the new ClipArt Gallery will be used by all your installed versions of Office. That is, if you choose to insert ClipArt into a Word 6 document, you will be presented with the Office version of ClipArt.

Another Selective Service

You can select text with the mouse, you can hold down Shift and use the arrow keys, you can double-click, triple-click, and you can click in the margin. Do you need another way to select text? Probably not, However, here it is anyway.

Click at the beginning of text you would like to select. Now look at the bottom of the Word window. See the Button marked EXT? Double-click EXT and it will become active (you will see this when it happens). Now you can use the arrow keys to select text. You do not have to hold down anything while you do this. When you are finished, press Esc.

Speeding Up Your Access Files

If you have a large database from which you primarily read data, you may never need to compact it. However, a database that you constantly write data to, and delete data from, will soon become extremely fragmented; and you may begin to notice that it does not run as fast as it did in the old days.

What you need to do is compact those fragmented Access database files. Here is how:
Close the database you want to compact. Choose Tools|Database Utilities|Compact Database. When the dialog box opens, select the file you want to compact, and Access will automatically assign a new name to the output file. Click on Compact and then click on Save to save your new compacted file.

If you want to save back to the original file name, you can make the change here (in the Save dialog box). Type in the new (original) name and click on Save. Access will warn you that you are about to overwrite your original file.

Color-code Your Tasks

You can color-code your tasks list to make it easy to see which tasks are overdue. To change the color of overdue and completed tasks, select Tools/Options, and click the Tasks/Notes tab. Under Task Color Options, choose colors from the drop-down menus to signify completed and overdue tasks, then click OK. Your tasks list will now be easier to read.

Drop-Down Forms

If you need to generate a form for people to fill in, you might want to consider using drop-down lists. This makes it easy for you to read the results because it forces certain responses of you are choosing--eliminating the possibility of answers that have nothing to do with the questions.

As an example, let us consider an age entry. You could ask for age and let people fill in the blank. However, if the age group is more important to you than a specific age, you can use a drop-down list.

First, choose View, Toolbars, and Forms to place the Forms toolbar in your Word window. Now click where you want the list to appear and then go to the toolbar and click on the Drop-Down Form Field Button (the icon resembles a drop-down list).

After you insert the form, click on the Form Field Options Button (it is the next Button to the right of the Drop-Down Form Field Button). When the dialog box opens, enter the first age group and click on Add. Repeat until all the age groups are entered. When you are finished, click on OK.

To get your form to work, click on the Protect Form Button (it looks like a padlock). To edit your form, click on the Protect Form Button again.

FTP 101

Do you upload or download a lot of files to and from FTP sites? Office's File Open dialog box does the job for you. Assuming you have TCP/IP running (that is, you are connected to the Internet), select File Open and click on the arrow next to the Look In box. Right at the bottom of the selections, you will see the option to add any FTP site you like, whether it is anonymous FTP or something that requires a password. You can even save your password for later use, if you wish.

Database Damage

No matter how careful we are with our databases, stuff happens-- the power might drop out, or the network might fail. For whatever reason, there are times when a damaged database is a distinct possibility. If you encounter a damaged Access database, choose Data/Database Utilities/Repair Database. When the dialog box opens, click on the errant file to select it, and then click on Repair. Access will let you know when it is finished.

Saving Normal.dot

Word has a template file called Normal.dot that is the basis for the default new, blank file. A number of people have experienced problems saving Normal.dot. Here is how it works. If you open Normal.dot, you can make changes and then save the file by choosing File|Save. If you start with a new document, make style changes, and then try to save the file as Normal.dot using File|Save As, Word will refuse to save the file. If you really need to do this, you can save the file as Normal2.dot and then later delete or rename the original Normal.dot and replace it with your new file by renaming Normal2.dot to Normal.dot.

Chapter 21

Quicken general

Reports and Classes

To create a class within a category (click on a transaction, press Ctrl-L, and add the classes). If you split a category into classes, you can show the individual classes in your reports by doing the following:

- Click on the Reports Button at the bottom of the Quicken window and choose Easy Answer Reports/Graphs.
- In the Easy Answer dialog box, choose the How Much Did I Spend On option and select the category from the drop-down list.
- Click on Show Report.
- To see an individual class, click on the Customize Button.
- Click on the arrow beside the Subtotal By list box to expand it.
- From this expanded list, select Class and click on Create.

You get a report that shows the expenditure in each class of the chosen category.

Make Your Reports More Attractive

Quicken enables you to generate some killer reports. However, you might not know that you can do quite a bit to change a report's appearance. For one thing, you may want to change the width of the columns to make all the headings display completely. To do this, follow these steps:

- With your report on-screen, locate the column markers (they are small diamond-shaped icons near the column headings).
- Place your mouse pointer over a marker; the pointer changes to crosshairs.
- Now you can use the mouse to drag the column border right or left to expand or contract it.

To change the typeface used in the headings and body text, do the following:

- Press Ctrl-P. In the Print dialog box, you see a Button for Heading font and another for Body Font.

- Click on whichever you want to change and make your selection.
- Click on OK to print.

do not forget The Debit Card

Modern technology has made it easier than ever to overdraw your checking account. We are referring to the debit card. This little monster lets you use your checking account to pay for items in places that would never take a check. The thing is, we often have trouble keeping track of the amounts we withdraw using the card. We suggest this: Always take care of the withdrawals as soon as you get home. Keep the receipts and consider them entries in a checkbook. If you are on vacation, try putting all your debit card receipts in an envelope, so when you get home you can enter them into Quicken. When you enter the amount withdrawn by a debit card, Quicken suggests that you select EFT (Electronic Funds Transfer) in the Num Field's drop-down list to help you keep track of how the money was withdrawn.

Another tip: Most ATM windows cast a nice reflection, affording a great opportunity to fix your hair or see if you dribbled any lunch on yourself. Try to ignore the little camera.

Shortcut Keys

- Ctrl + O to open a file
- Ctrl + B to back up a file
- Ctrl + P to print a file
- Ctrl + N to start a new account
- Ctrl + W to write a check
- Ctrl + A to open the account list
- Ctrl + T to get to the memorized transaction list
- Ctrl + K to open the calendar
- Ctrl + R to open a register
- Ctrl + H to open a loan window

- Ctrl + C to open a category list
- Ctrl + J to open scheduled transactions
- F1 to get help on the current window

Credit Worthy

Contrary to what most people think, a direct relationship exists between credit cards and actual money. Eventually, you are going to have to actually pay for the stuff you buy with credit cards. If you are a bit credit card happy (in addition;, really, who is not?), you may want to set up and use a separate credit card account. Doing so not only hand les paying your credit card bills, However, it can help you keep close track of what you owe. To set up a separate credit card account, follow these steps:

- Choose Lists + Account (or press Ctrl-A).
- When the Account List appears, click on New.
- Select Credit Card and click on Next.
- Enter an Account name and description, and click on Next.
- If you have your last statement (you will need it eventually), select Yes; then click on Next.
- Enter the statement date and the balance and then click on Next.
- If your card is not from Quicken and you do not use Online banking, select No and then click on Next.
- Enter the cards credit limit and click on Next.
- The Account summary appears. If all is well, click on Done.
- Back in the account list; double-click on your new entry to get to the Register.

Assuming you have a checking account already set up, when you make a credit card payment, choose Transfer To/From Checking. This way, the payment is automatically subtracted from your checking account.

Tracking Mutual Funds

Quicken offers a hand y way to track your mutual funds. (However, before you start tracking your mutual funds, ask yourself whether you really need to. For example, you do not need to track an IRA or a 401K invested in mutual funds. As tax-free transactions, all you have to do is subtract the contributions ions from your pretax income.) For those mutual funds you do want to track, you first have to set up an account:

- Choose Lists + Account and click on New.
- Select Investment and click on Next.
- Enter your account name and a description (if desired) and click on Next.
- In response to the check-writing prompt, select No and click on Next.
- Select One Mutual Fund and click on Next.
- Unless you are tracking a tax-deferred account, click on No and then click on Next.
- When the Summary screen appears, select Account Contains a Single Mutual Fund.
- Click on Done. Quicken will create the new Register.
- Double-click on your new entry to open the Register.

Now you can start entering the data--purchase price, shares, dollar amounts, and so on--for your mutual fund investments.

The Truth Can Hurt

In the last tip, we explained how to open and view Snapshots (Reports + Snapshots). This time, we show you how to customize Snapshot to make it look the way you want it to look:

- Choose Reports + Snapshots.
- Click on Customize.
- Under the Snapshot Type listing, choose the type of snapshot you would like to see. The list includes many very useful data,

such as charts comparing your monthly income and expenses over a period of time and actual vs. budgeted income.

- Click on OK.

To close Snapshot, click on the Close box at the upper right corner of the Snapshot window.

Using Graphs

Graphs are a good way to view your transactions because they provide you with a visual display of where your money has gone. Sometimes when numbers do not have a big impact, graphs do. For example, you can view or print a report showing all your expenditures for the year, However, there are many numbers to view. On the other hand, if you create a graphic view, you can see immediately where all your money has gone--as in, "We spent THAT much of our money on candy?" To view a graph of your expenditures to date, do the following:

- Click on Reports and choose Easy Answer Reports/Graphs.
- When the dialog box opens, click on Show Graph.

That is quite a candy budget you have there!

Auto start Quicken

Remember when you were a schoolchild and you had a big crush on that kid who sat behind you? How you could not wait to see him or her first thing in the morning? Now that you are all grown up, do you feel that way about Quicken. If so, you should seek help. In the meantime, if you run Windows 95 and use Quicken every day, you may want to have it start automatically, as soon as Windows 95 opens. What could be better? You turn on the computer, and there is Quicken. If you like this idea, here is how to set it up.

- Close Quicken.
- Run Windows Explorer.
- Locate the Windows folder.
- Click on the plus sign on the left of the folder to open it.
- Locate the Start Menu folder.
- Click on its plus sign.
- Locate Programs.
- Click on its plus sign.
- Click on Quicken.
- Use the mouse to drag Quicken 6 for Windows to the Startup folder.
- Click on the Close box at the upper right corner of the Explorer window (it looks like an X).

Now when you turn on your computer, Quicken will be there waiting for you.

Make Your Own NUM Selection

In a previous tip, we made some comments about how to deal with debit card s, those magic card s that make it so easy to become destitute. Quicken suggests that you assign EFT to the Num field. However, you might not find the entry EFT to your liking. Fortunately, Quicken is so flexible that it lets you create another field called Debit or something more sensible. If you would prefer that your debit card entries display Debit in the Num field, rather than EFT, try this:

- Click in the Num field to expand the list.
- Click on Edit List.
- Click on New.
- Enter Debit.
- Click on OK.
- Click on Done.

Now you can select Debit in the Num field when you enter a debit card   transaction.

Register Navigation

When a register begins to get large, think about the time it takes just to navigate through the thing--probably not the most efficient use of your time. To help you out, here are a few shortcuts that you can use to get around in a register more quickly:

- To move up one screen, press Page Up.
- To move down one screen, press Page Down.
- To get to the first transaction, click on the Date field and press Ctrl-Home.
- To get to the last transaction, click on the Date field and press Ctrl-End.

Stay Balanced

Unless you are Mary Poppins, the time will come, and more often than you would like, when your account will not balance. This is less likely to happen when you use Quicken than when you simply scribble numbers into your checkbook, However, it still happens. To balance an account:

- Choose Features + Banking + Reconcile.
- In the Choose Reconcile Account dialog box, choose the account you want to reconcile and click on OK.
- In the next screen, enter the ending balance.
- Enter any service charges, or interest if applicable.
- Click on OK.
- Now click on each transaction that has cleared (a checkmark will appear).
- If the Difference is zero, you are OK.
- Click on Finish.

If there is a discrepancy, go through all your numbers to look for the error.

See It All

How would you like to get a quick overview of all your financial dealings for the year--all at once? You can:

• Choose Reports + Snapshots to open a snapshot collection of graphs and reports, a sort of mini-view of everything Quicken can find to show.
• To see a larger view of any of the items, click on the item you want to enlarge and then click on Enlarge.
• To get back to the original view, click on the Close box (the X in the upper right corner of the current window).

A Graphics Primer

When you use graphics to view your income and expenses, you need to make sure that you choose the right graph and the right layout to match your requirements. For example, if you want to show all the expenses, you do not want a 3D pie chart because the small expenses do not display properly. Take a look at an example:

1. Temporarily create a small transaction--say $5.95.
2. Choose Reports + Graphs + Income and Expenses
3. Click on Create.
4. Look at both graphs--bar and pie. Can you see the small transaction?
5. Click on Options.
6. Select Draw in 2D

The small transaction shows up better in 2D. However, take a look at the bar chart: It does not have enough resolution to display the small transaction. Although chances are you will not generally have such a small amount in a single category, you should be aware that not all graphs can show all transactions equally well.

Chapter 22

Keeping Desktop & Start Menu Clean general

We have seen this too often. A user places all his 'stuff' on to his desktop or start menu. As a result, it is too messy and becomes so cluttered that even the user has trouble finding what he/she is looking for.

A Clean Desktop

Place only your most frequently used programs on to the desktop. Always place shortcuts <u>and not</u> the program itself onto the desktop. You can however, place folders which is a convenience on the desktop. Try not to fill up more than 3/4 of the desktop. If you place too many items onto the desktop, windows will place them beyond the screen and you will have to use the desktop folder itself instead. You will also have trouble using desktop components as they are all covered with icons. If you have a set of utilities, you will like to have access to, use toolbars as a quick alternative. Set them to auto-hide to free up the desktop.

A Clean Start Menu

Dump your start menu shortcuts into manageable folders. Put all you games into one folder. Place all your stand -alone system utilities under System Tools. Group all your MS Office applications under another folder. You get what we mean. It will clear up the start menu and you will not have to scroll to the bottom just to launch a program. If you have a lot of first-level items on your start menu, use small icons instead by right-clicking the Taskbar Properties.

Chapter 23

Setting Up Your Keyboard general

Click on the Accessibility Options icon on your Control Panel. On the Keyboard tab, you will see some certain settings. This setting might not be just for those who are having trouble using the Keyboard only. You can also use it to benefit you for better performance.

StickyKeys

Say that you have trouble pressing several keys at once such as the Ctrl, Shift, or Alt keys. Use this option for your convenience. You can set it to display StickyKey on status too.

FilterKeys

If you want Windows to ignore the brief delay or repeated keystrokes. This can prevent you from accidentally repeating the same keystroke. Or better still, you can make you PC beep when it accepted your keystroke.

ToggelKeys

Some of you sometimes pressed the Caps Lock key when you actually want to use the Tab key without realizing it. To prevent this from happening, use ToggelKeys to make your PC beep when you press the Caps Lock, Num Lock, or Scroll Lock keys.

MouseKey

Click on the Mouse tab. MouseKey is useful for laptops or people with difficulty with the mouse; you can use the numeric pad to control the cursor. However, it can be really useful when it comes to imaging programs where you want to move exactly just a few pixels. The MouseKey is one of our favorites.

Chapter 24

Keyboard Shortcuts For Lefties

There is nothing wrong with being a left-hand ed. After all, lefties are supposed to be more creative and clever. However, you will find it a pain when you want to use the Cut, Copy, Paste Keyboard shortcuts. Ctrl-X, Ctrl-C & Ctrl-V are only accessible in the left hand. Since you are using the mouse on the left hand, will not it be better if there is a shortcut for it in the right-hand side of the Keyboard?

However, there is! Remember the entire old Keyboard shortcut in DOS? It still works with most application under Windows (not under Windows itself though).

For Right-Handers
Cut: Ctrl +X
Copy: Ctrl+C
Paste: Ctrl+V
Undo: Ctrl+Z

For Left-Handers
Cut: Shift-Delete
Copy: Ctrl-Insert

Paste: Shift-Insert
Undo: Alt-Backspace

Sadly, not all applications work with these shortcuts. Experiment yourself whether your applications works with it or not.

Chapter 25

What Is The Registry general

The Registry is a hierarchical database within later versions of Windows (95/98/NT4/NT5) where all the system settings are stored. It has replaced all of the .ini files that were present in Windows 3.x. The data from system.ini, win.ini, control.ini, are all contained within it now, along with hundreds of other system settings. Additionally, all Windows specific programs are now to store their initialization data within the Registry instead of in .ini files in your Windows folder.

About The Registry Editor

The Registry cannot be viewed or edited with a normal editor - you must use a program included with Windows called RegEdit (Registry editor) for Windows 95 & 98 or RegEdit32 for Windows NT 4 & 5. This program is not listed on your Start Menu and it is well hidden in your Windows directory. To run this program, just click on Start, Run, and type regedit (for Win 9x) or regedit32 (for Win NT) in the input field. This will start the Registry Editor. Now add this to the Start Menu or to the desktop for easier editing.

Foreword

As we have introduced in our previous page, the Registry cannot be viewed or edited with a normal editor - you may only use the

Registry Editor. This program is not listed on your Start Menu and it is well hidden in your Windows directory. To run this program, just click on Start, Run, and type regedit (for Win 9x) or regedit32 (for Win NT) in the input field. Press Enter.

As we have introduced the keys and strings in our previous page, now we will focus on editing the Registry using the Registry Editor. We realized that the help file included together with the Registry Editor is not very helpful. If you were to print it out, it will consume only about 2 and a half page. We will try our best to fill in what that is not mentioned in the help file.

Editing With The Registry Editor

First, a slight tutorial. The Registry editor is divided into 2 panes. The left pane is a tree structure of keys while the right pane shows the string values the selected branch contains (you will learn more on strings and their values later on). When you right-click on a key, the menu as shown above will appear.

Expand: Expand the branch
New   : Create a new key or string value
Find   : Find a selected key or string value
Delete   : Delete the entire highlighted item
Rename: Rename the highlighted item
Copy Key Name: (only available in OSR2 versions and above)
Copy out the key name (with current key name location).

Always use the Registry Editor with care. There are 3 very dangerous things about the Registry Editor.

1. What is done is done. There is not any Undo option available. In case you accidentally deleted a key, it is gone for good.
2. When you edit the Registry, all changes will be saved instantly, you do not have the option to "reload" the registry in case you have done something wrong.

3.   You never know when you have done something wrong. There will be no warning pop-out dialogue boxes telling stating you have deleted a vital key. The Registry Editor will let you wipe clean everything without giving you a warning.

Third-Party Registry Editors

Although the Windows Registry Editor seems good enough, if you have any third party registry editors like the one included in Norton Utilities, use it! It can make no difference if you are an expert However, if you are a beginner, the editors actually offers you more information and better understand and towards s the Registry. And these editors actually offer you an Undo option (hurray!).

Importance Of Backing Up The Registry

It is very vital to back up your Registry, is not it? It makes sense since the Registry is such an important thing. Without it, Windows will not load properly. The Registry editor is able to Import and Export the registry for storage and backup. The whole registry will usually take about 800 kb, enough to fit into a diskette.

.REG Files

To make importing and exporting easier, the Registry editor includes an easy way to do it which involves .reg files. These files are known as "Registry Entries" where registry data is stored in it. These files are actually in ASCII format where you can view it with any text-editors. You can double-click the file and all the data in the file will "merge" into the registry - which is why it is dangerous. There is no way to unmerge it when the deed is done. Always be very careful.

Exporting Registry Keys

It is very vital to back up your Registry, is not it? It makes sense since the Registry is such an important thing. There is not "Save As" function in the Registry Editor, which means you cannot just choose to save it as a file. However, you can choose to Export your registry to a file. First, click on File, Export Registry File. You can choose whether you to back up the whole Registry (recommended if you have not backed up the Registry) with the All option or Selected branch for only the highlighted branch.

Note that there is no way to export a selected Value. The least you can do is backup the entire branch (key). That means the other values will also be backed up. If you want to export only a few keys, export it to a .reg file first than edit with your text-editor to delete unnecessary keys.

Importing Registry Keys

This is similar to the "Load" commanding a different twist. The Import Registry File will take the selected file, read it and place all the data in the file and merge it into the Registry. The Registry editor will replace existing keys in the Registry and create non-existing keys with the ones in the file. Always make sure you have the right file before you begin

The Registry Files

As a centralized database of your system's configuration settings, you might be wondering where is the Registry stored after numerous finds for a large .reg file. Amazingly, the Registry is actually made up of two separate files: USER.DAT and SYSTEM.DAT. The USER.DAT file contains information specific to the user, while SYSTEM.DAT contains information specific to the system. The reason that the Registry divides its database into two separate files is to simplify network administration. However, we mention these filenames because each time you start Windows 95 successfully, it backs up these two files, thus backing up the

Registry. Windows 95 backs up USER.DAT as USER.DA0 and SYSTEM.DAT as SYSTEM.DA0.

If you made a mistake on the Registry and Windows will not boot properly, Windows will not back up the two files, which means there is still a good copy of your Registry on the last successful boot up. This means you can restore the system by copying the backups over the corrupted files if Windows fails to start after you have made changes to the Registry.

You will find both the DAT and DA0 files in your Windows 95 folder. However, if you have created a user profile, you will find the two USER files in the Profiles folder. You can easily track down any of the files using Windows 95's Find utility.

Restoring A Corrupted Registry

Now for the hard part. In any case, Windows will not start because of registry errors we have a cure. Go to CommandPrompt via the F8 menu. On the commandprompt, type

```
cd c:\windows
attrib -h -r -s system.dat
attrib -h -r -s user.dat
attrib -h -r -s system.da0
attrib -h -r -s user.da0
copy user.da0 system.dat
copy user.da0 user.dat
```

Windows will restore the Registry the way it is on the last successful boot. We recommend you to copy this into a .txt file in case you cannot remember the command. This can be viewed with the Edit utility under DOS.

Interface

Disable ToolTips

Although ToolTips may be helpful, you might find it annoying. To disable it, go to HKEY_USERS\.DEFAULT\Control Panel\Desktop. On the right pane, double-click UserPreferencemask and change the value to 3E 00 00 00. To enable it again, change the value back to BE 00 00 00.

Turn Off Windows Zooming Animation

The windows zooming animation probably originated from Mac OS's. It is considered one of the cute features of window. However, if you have plenty of windows to maximize and minimize, you will wish there is not such a feature. Open up the registry editor and go to HKEY_CURRENT_USER\Control Panel\desktop\. On the right pane, look for a value called MinAnimate. Change the value to 0. Restart Windows and the animation are gone.

Editing Menu Pop/Slide Out Speed

When you pass your mouse over a menu, you will notice that there is a slight delay before the submenu pops out (Windows 95, NT4) or slide out (Windows98, NT5). Now this is suppose to be a feature from Microsoft for new Windows users to look "friendly". Now there are 2 groups of people who will get very annoyed. The first one is the ones who think that the delay is not needed. They want the menu to fly out instantaneously. The second line are the ones who do not want the menu to pop out when you pass your mouse over them - they want them to pop out only when you click at the menu like old DOS and Win 3.11 menus.

Open up the registry editor and go to HKEY_CURRENT_USER\Control Panel\Desktop\ On the right pane, and look for a value called MenuShowDelay. If it is not there, just create one. Now, to set the value in milliseconds. Now, we have seen a lot of books and sites saying that the value should be set to 1 for fastest and 10 for slowest. Wrong! Since the value is set to milliseconds, a little calculation will tell you that the figures do not make any sense. The default is 400 (see? 1-10 is way off the track). Set 50 or below for fast or near instant fly-out or 65534 for near eternity. Since we cannot disable the menu to fly out when you mouse over them, you can set them to the maximum value so that they will not pop out until a long time. Click on the menu for them to pop out.

However, we noticed that if you use the "click once to select" in addition", highlight when pointing" option, you would find that this registry tip would affect your mouse. If you set the menu delay to very fast, you will notice that the brief delay of highlighting icon is gone (hurray!). However, if you set the menu delay to almost never, your icon highlighting will also be gone! You will have to click once to highlight and click again to activate the icon.

Aligning Drop-Down Menus to the Right

All Windows' drop-down menus will be aligned to the left of the menu item itself. It is possible to align it to the right instead. This feature becomes useful when trying to access menus with submenus that appear directly to the right.

Open up the registry editor and go to HKEY_CURRENT_USER\Control Panel\Desktop. On the right pane, create a string entry called MenuDropAlignment. Set its value to 1. Restart and you will notice that now all the drop-down menus are aligned to the right.

Editing Inaccessible Appearance Items

You can change the appearance of Windows in your Control Panel, Display applet or right-click your desktop and select Properties. However, there are still some things you just cannot change. For example, you might find it tempting to change your disabled (grayed out), highlighted, or shadowed object. Never mind that, just open your registry editor, and go to HKEY_CURRENT_USER \Control Panel\Colors. On the right pane are the display options in RGB triplets. Search for keys with highlight or shadow descriptions.

Chapter 26

Start Menu general

Remove Run From Start Menu

To remove the Run command from the Start Menu,

Fire up the registry editor.
Go to
HKEY_CURRENT_USER\Software\Microsoft\Windows\Current Version\Policies\Explorer
Double-click NoRun on the right pane and change it to from 0 to 1.
To restore the Run command, reverse the steps by changing 1 to 0.

Remove Favorites From Start Menu

If you think you really do not need the favorites menu, follow the steps to remove it.

Flare up registry editor.
Scroll to
HKEY_CURRENT_USER\Software\Microsoft\Windows\Current Version\Policies\Explorer
Right-click on the right pane and select New, DWORD Value.
Name it NoFavoritesMenu.
Double-click and enter 1 as value. To restore the Favorites menu, reverse the steps by changing 1 to 0 or delete DWORD value.

Remove Documents From Start Menu

The Documents menu is a nuisance for those who never actually used it.

To remove, launch registry editor.
Scroll to
HKEY_CURRENT_USER\Software\Microsoft\Windows\ Current Version\Policies\Explorer
Right-click on the right pane and select New, DWORD Value.
Name it NoRecentDocsMenu.
Double-click and enter 1 as value. To restore the Documents menu, reverse the steps by changing 1 to 0 or delete DWORD value.

Remove Log Off User From Start Menu

For those of you who do not need the Log Off User option, these are the steps to remove it.

Flare up registry editor.
Scroll to
HKEY_CURRENT_USER\Software\Microsoft\Windows\Current Version\Policies\Explorer
Right-click on the right pane and select New, DWORD Value.
Name it NoLogOff.
Double-click and enter 1 as value. To restore the Log Off User option, reverse the steps by changing 1 to 0 or delete DWORD value.

Remove Find From Start Menu

If you already have a better search program and want to disable the one in the Start Menu, here is how to remove it.

Launch the registry editor.
Scroll to

HKEY_CURRENT_USER\Software\Microsoft\Windows\Current Version\Policies\Explorer

Right-click on the right pane and select New, DWORD Value. Name it NoFind.

Double-click and enter 1 as value. Note: This will also disable the Find under Explorer and will not respond to the F3 key. To restore the Log Off User option, reverse the steps by changing 1 to 0 or delete DWORD value.

Remove Windows Update From Settings

There will be a Windows Update item at the Settings branch of the Start Menu. To get remove it, flare up the registry editor and go to HKEY_CURRENT_USER\Software\Microsoft\Windows\Current Version\Policies\Explorer. Create a new Binary value called NoWindowsUpdate. Set the value to 01 00 00 00.. To restore, change the value of the key to 00 00 00 00.

Remove Active Desktop From Settings

To remove the Active Desktop submenu item from the Settings branch of the Start Menu, use the registry editor and go to HKEY_CURRENT_USER\Software\Microsoft\Windows\Current Version\Policies\Explorer. Create a new Binary value called NoSetActiveDesktop. Set the value to 01 00 00 00.. To restore, change the value of the key to 00 00 00 00.

Remove Taskbar From Settings

To remove the Taskbar submenu item from the Settings branch of the Start Menu, use the registry editor and go to HKEY_CURRENT_USER\Software\Microsoft\Windows\Current Version\Policies\Explorer. Create a new Binary value called NoSetTaskbar. Set the value to 01 00 00 00.. To restore, change the value of the key to 00 00 00 00.

Remove Folder Options From Settings

To remove the Folder Options submenu item from the Settings branch of the Start Menu, use the registry editor and go to HKEY_CURRENT_USER\Software\Microsoft\Windows\Current Version\Policies\Explorer. Create a new Binary value called NoSetFolders . Set the value to 01 00 00 00.. To restore, change the value of the key to 00 00 00 00.

Restore Start Menu To Alphabetical Order

We always liked the alphabetical order of the Start Menu. It will help organize things. However, we noticed that with IE4 (and Windows 98), Windows will arrange all items that are in the Start Menu in alphabetical order first during installation. Observe and you will see that all single items will be placed below all folders.

Now for the problem. You will also notice that after the installation of Windows, all new folders added will be placed below the single items that come with Windows. This means that there will be 3 sections, one for folders, one for single items and another one for new folders after installation. Wondering why Windows cannot just group all the folders together in alphabetical order However, to put new folders apart from the old ones after install?

We found that the answer lies in the registry. Open your registry editor and go to HKEY_CURRENT_USER\Software\Microsoft\Windows\Current Version\Explorer\MenuOrder\Start Menu Click once on Menu and on the right pane, you will see a string value named Order. Double-click this value. On the right side, you will see a list of folder and shortcut names this string was created during install to record all folders and shortcuts. All new entries added after install will be recorded in the end of the value rather than placing them in the middle of the key which is why, although all new folders created

129

will be placed in alphabetical order too However, not together with the folders after setup.

The workaround is simple - just delete the Order value and the registry will create a new one without any order. Since the registry has lost all records on how the start menu should be arranged, restart and you will see that the start menu has been rearranged in alphabetical order - together.

This tip works on the entire Start Menu branch. Another branch that has also the "record" thing is the Accessories branch. Repeat the same step.

More Start Button Fun

Let us say you have about 4-5 very useful applications which you use always. By placing them, all on the first level menu will eventually crowd your start menu. Now why not utilize the right-click option instead? The right-click option gives you the ability to Open, Explore and Find. If you can add a shortcut to your application to that menu, it would be great.

To do this, crank up your registry editor and go to HKEY_CLASSES_ROOT\Directory\Shell. Right-click on Shell and creates a new key. Type in an appropriate name for the key. On the right pane, double-click on the Default value, and add a title with a & character in front of the letter as an accelerator key. Right-click on the key you just created and create another key under it called command. For the Default value of command, enter the full path and program you want to execute in the Value data box.

For example, if you wanted Notepad, you would add that as the first key, the default in the right panel would be &Notepad so when you right click on the Start Button, the N would be underlined, and you could just press that key. The commin addition would be something like C:\Windows\notepad.exe. Now when you right click on the Start Button, your new program will show up

Chapter 27

Explorer general

BMP Thumbnail As Icon

You can actually use a thumbnail version of a BMP file for its own icon displayed in Explorer. Go to HKCU\Paint.Picture\Default. Double-click default and change its value to %1. Please note however that this will slow down the display rate in explorer if there are too many BMP thumbnails to display. To restore it, change default back to C:\Progra~1\Access~1\MSPAINT.EXE,1. You may use other icons if you feel like it.

Default Icon Display

Most of uses are not so satisfied with the default icon view. A little tweak on the registry can cure that. Open up your registry editor and get ready.

Control Panel Icon Display

The default icon view for windows such as the control panel, windows opened with the "Open" command on the context menu, and similar windows can be changed by modifying the registry. Go to this key: HKEY_CURRENT_USER\Software\Microsoft\Windows\Current Version\Explorer\Streams On the right panel, there is an entry like this: 03,00,00,00,03,00,00,00 and the fifth group of numbers controls the icons.

Large icons = 01
Small icons = 02
List = 03
Details = 04

Place the cursor to the left of the fifth position, hit delete and then enter the new value.

Explorer Icon Display

Like the above tip, the default icon view that displays in the right panel of the Explorer can also be changed by modifying the registry. Open up HKEY_CURRENT_
USER\ Software\Microsoft\Windows\CurrentVersion\Explorer\Ex pView. Highlight ExpView. On the tool bar, click Registry and select Export Registry File. This brings up a save screen where you name the file and direct where it is filed when saved. Edit the exported file. There are three lines of data in the data stream. There are 21 bytes of data in the first line and 25 bytes of data in the second. The 45th byte of data (the next to last in line two) controls how the icons are displayed. Refer to the above paragraph for entering the new icon display value. After making a change, save the file and close it. Then double click the file to merge it into the registry.

Save Window Settings

Funny why you have customized the look (toolbars, view, details) of an Explorer or Control Panel window only to find that the second window does not look the same as the one you have just customized. However, there are ways to have your Explorer/Control Panel window keep its settings for good. Start your registry editor and go to HKEY_CURRENT_USER\Software\Microsoft\Windows\Current Version\Policies\Explorer. In the right hand pane, you will find the NoSaveSetting key. No matter what value is given to this Registry key, the Desktop/Explorer/Control Panel settings will still be modified again after opening 29 of those windows. Delete the NoSaveSettings key. Just refresh your desktop to take effect.

Make DLL Files Show Their Own Icons

If you find the generic Control Panel Applets or DLL old icon with the two gears boring, something can be done.

Fire up your registry editor and go to HKEY_CLASSES_ROOT\cplfile\DefaultIcon. Change the default string value to %1. This for Control Panel icons. For DLLs, go to HKEY_CLASSES_ROOT\dllfile\DefaultIcon and change the default string value to %1.

The next time you take a look at your C:\Windows\System directory, you will see that old icon with the two gears, any DLLs and Control Panel applets (CPLs) that contain even one icon will show something more interesting--the first icon they contain. The only drawback is that the "unknown type" icon represents DLLs and CPLs that do not contain icons. However, you might just think it is worth it.

Customizing The Shortcut Arrow

Windows will attach a black arrow to icons to distinguish shortcuts from the original. Most of us just find this more annoying than helpful. Most tipsters will advice you to search the registry for a value called Piffile and delete every instances of it. However, we find that it is impossible to recover it when the deed is done. We have another trick with a little twist.

Open up your registry editor and go to HKEY_LOCAL_MACHINE\SOFTWARE\Microsoft\Windows\CurrentVersion\explorer\Shell Icons. Now, on the right pane is a list of icons (we found out that on some systems, Windows 98 especially, the right pane is blank. do not worry; just add the value as required). Find the value 29. If it is not there, just add it. The value of this string should be C:\Windows\system\shell32.dll, 29 (which means the 30th icon in shell32.dll - the first one begins with 0). Now, we need blank icon to do this. Just create one with white as the whole icon. Go here to learn how to create an icon. Once done just change the value to C:\xxx.ico, 0 where "xxx" is the full path of the icon file and "0" is the icon in it.

Now for some fun. If the blank icon is a bit boring, change it again. You will find that under shell32.dll there is a gear icon, a shared folder (the hand) and much more. Experiment for yourself!

Remove The "Shortcut To" Prefix

Is the "Shortcut to" text prefix on your shortcuts annoying you no end? Here is the way to remove all instances from all your shortcuts.

Fire up your registry editor and go to HKEY_USERS\.Default\Software\Microsoft\Windows\CurrentVersion\Explorer. On the left pane, create a new binary value named link. Set the value to 00 00 00 00. Restart your system and the "Shortcut To" text prefix is gone.

Note: This applies to all you exist as well as and newly added shortcuts!

Enable or Disable the CD-ROM Autorun Feature

You can disable the CD-ROM autorun by changing this setting; this will stop applications from auto launching when you insert a CD-ROM disc into your drive.

Open:
HKEY_LOCAL_MACHINE\SYSTEM\CurrentControlSet\Service
s\CDRom

Change to value of 'Autorun', or create a new DWORD value if it
does not exist: (0=disable, 1=enable)

Restart Your Computer.

Chapter 28

Desktop general

Wallpaper Position

Windows 95 with Plus installed and Windows 98 offer 2 ways to
align your wallpaper - "Center" or "tiled" and "Stretch to fit the
desktop". However, there is an undocumented way to align your
wallpaper at any position by specifying X and Y coordinates.

Fire up your registry editor and go to
HKEY_CURRENT_USER\Control Panel\Desktop. Create 2 new
strings and call them WallpaperOriginX and WallpaperOriginY
respectively With the keys now up, just set the value along
coordinate X and Y to position your wallpaper in pixels.

More Flexibility For Desktop Icons

If you are the one who does not want to waste, you might be
making use of all the icons on the desktop. Our last tip did not
make any effect on you since you have no intention of deleting any
of them. However, would you like more flexibility for these "stiff"
system icons?

Refer to our last tip for searching the CLSID for the system icons. Then go to

HKEY_CLASSES_ROOT\CLSID\{xxxxxxxx-xxxx-xxxx-xxxx-xxxxxxxxxxxx}

where xxxxxxxx-xxxx-xxxx-xxxx-xxxxxxxxxxxx is the icon's CLSID.

Now, on the right-frame, search for a value called AttriHowever, es. If the value is not available, that means that you can edit on that icon and it must be left alone. If it is there, change the value to 70 01 00 20.

Back to the desktop, you can now do impossible things on the icons like rename or even delete the Recycle Bin!

Remove Pesky Desktop Icons

There are some annoying icons that sitting on your desktop that you find you do not even touched at all. Removing some of these cannot be any better. The easy way is to make a few Registry changes. Run your registry editor, and go to HKEY_CURRENT_USER\Software\Microsoft\Windows\Current Version\Policies\Explorer.

Let us say you want to remove the "Network Neighborhood" icon. With the above key highlighted, right click anywhere in the Registry field, select New, and click DWORD, to create a new entry. Name it NoNetHood When you set its value to 1 and then reboot, the Network Neighborhood desktop icon will be gone! To restore this icon on your desktop, change its value to 0. The good thing about this trick is that you can apply it to all your Desktop system icons.

To make changes to any other unwanted icon, go to:

HKEY_LOCAL_MACHINE\SOFTWARE\Microsoft\Windows\C
urrentVersion\explorer\Desktop\NameSpace{xxxxxxxx-xxxx-
xxxx-xxxx-xxxxxxxxxxxx}.

Within this key, each system icon has its own CLSID key (Class
ID), a 16-byte value, which identifies an individual object) that
points to a corresponding key in the Registry:

HKEY_CLASSES_ROOT\CLSID{xxxxxxxx-xxxx-xxxx-xxxx-
xxxxxxxxxxxx}

To delete an icon, remove the 16 byte CLSID value within
NameSpace. To change an icon name, change the value of its sister
CLSID key:

HKEY_CLASSES_ROOT\CLSID{xxxxxxxx-xxxx-xxxx-xxxx-
xxxxxxxxxxxx}\DefaultIcon

Therefore, the Network Neighborhood correspondent keys would
be:

HKEY_LOCAL_MACHINE\SOFTWARE\Microsoft\Windows\C
urrentVersion\explorer\Desktop\NameSpace\{208D2C60-3AEA-
1069-A2D7-08002B30309D}

and respectively:

KEY_CLASSES_ROOT\CLSID\{208D2C60-3AEA-1069-A2D7-
08002B30309D}

Here are the CLSID keys for all Windows 95/98/NT system icons:

- Briefcase {85BBD920-42A0-1069-A2E4-08002B30309D}
- Desktop {00021400-0000-0000-C000-000000000046}
- Control Panel {21EC2020-3AEA-1069-A2DD-
08002B30309D}

- Dial-Up Networking {992CFFA0-F557-101A-88EC-00DD010CCC48}
- Fonts {BD84B380-8CA2-1069-AB1D-08000948F534}
- Inbox {00020D76-0000-0000-C000-000000000046}
- The Internet {FBF23B42-E3F0-101B-8488-00AA003E56F8}
- My Computer {20D04FE0-3AEA-1069-A2D8-08002B30309D}
- Network Neighborhood {208D2C60-3AEA-1069-A2D7-08002B30309D}
- Printers {2227A280-3AEA-1069-A2DE-08002B30309D}
- Recycle Bin {645FF040-5081-101B-9F08-00AA002F954E}
- The Microsoft Network {00028B00-0000-0000-C000-000000000046}
- Url History Folder {FF393560-C2A7-11CF-BFF4-444553540000}

You can use the method above for any system icon you want to modify/delete. Go to the CLSID key you want to modify and change its Default Icon subkey. Recycle Bin makes an exception, its "Default" value lists the full pathname of the file that contains the corresponding icon. However, the easy way out to change the icons of My Computer, Network Neighborhood or Recycle Bin is the Plus! tab (Windows 95) or Effects (Windows 98) on the Display settings

We personally do not recommend you to remove the My Computer icon. It will cause you some system instability. Try our next tip to make a better use out of My Computer.

Boot Up

Searching For Start-up Programs

You have searched for them at the StartUp folder. You have search for them in your System.ini file. Yet still no instances of the annoying programs that loads at startup. Simple, some of them are still stored in the registry. Go to HKEY_CURRENT_USER\Software\Microsoft\Windows\Current Version. Under that, there are 2 keys named Run & RunOnce. Another place is HKEY_LOCAL_MACHINE\SOFTWARE\Microsoft\Windows\Current Version. Under that branch, search for keys named Run, RunOnce, RunOnceEx, RunServices & RunServicesOnce.

Once you find it, it is advisable not to delete the string. Instead, just clear away the value. Nicely done!

Turn NumLock On Or Off

Most of you have no problem turning the NumLock key on or off. All you need to do is to add a NUMLOCK=ON/OFF to your config.sys. However, if you boot to DOS 7 first (that is Windows without the UI shell) you might want DOS to have NumLock off while Windows to turn NumLock on or vice versa. This is virtually impossible because both Windows & DOS share the same Config.sys. There is a workaround to this problem though. Set the setting you want for DOS in your Config.sys file. Then use the registry to change the setting under Windows. To make this setting work, open your registry editor and go to HKEY_CURRENT_USER\ControlPanel\Microsoft\Input Devices. Right-click on Input Devices, then select New, Key. Name the new key Keyboard. Highlight Keyboard, right-click on it, and then click New, String Value. Name it NumLock. Enter ON as the value to turn the NumLock key on or OFF to turn it off.

Chapter 29

Internet Explorer general

Change Default Search Engine

To change the default Web search engine that IE 4 opens when you select Find|On the Internet from the Start menu, run Regedit and go to HKEY_CURRENT_USER\Software\Microsoft\Internet Explorer\Main. Double-click on SearchPage and enter the URL of the new search engine in the Value Data box.

Resizable Full Screen Toolbar

The full screen option is a real good idea. For most of us who do not need the toolbar, just set the autohide function on and the toolbar will be out of sight. However, there are also some of us who just want to resize the toolbar - a feature removed from IE after the beta phrase. So are we stuck with a non-resizable toolbar?

Not really, we have a registry hack to do this. However, since it utilizes binary values, we have decided to make it into a .reg file for easier use. Just copy the text below, paste it into Notepad and save it with a .reg extension. Double-click this file in addition you are done.

Toolbars

Older versions of Internet Explorer made it incredibly easy to move and resize toolbars -- maybe a little too easy. They seemed to get up and relocate magically. However, now that you have IE 6 you cannot seem to get them to budge.

- Unlock your toolbar
  1. Right-click the toolbar.
  2. Uncheck Lock the Toolbars.

- Move your toolbar
  1. Click the vertical line on the left side of each toolbar.
  2. Drag and drop the toolbar where you want it to appear.
- Lock toolbars in place
  1. Right-click the toolbar.
  2. Click Lock the Toolbars.

Printout of all your Favorites

If you want a printout of all your Favorites in Internet Explorer, you have to export them as an HTML file.

1. In Internet Explorer, click on File and select Import and Export.
2. A wizard starts. Follow along, remembering to export Favorites.
3. After the wizard completes the task, file the HTML file. It is probably in My Documents.
4. Open the file in Internet Explorer.
5. Click on the File menu and select Print.
6. On the Options tab, check "Print table of links."

REGEDIT4

```
[HKEY_CURRENT_USER\Software\Microsoft\Internet Explorer\Toolbar]
"Theater"=hex:0c,00,00,00,4c,00,00,00,74,00,00,00,18,00,00,00,1
b,00,00,00,5c,\

00,00,00,01,00,00,00,e0,00,00,00,a0,0f,00,00,05,00,00,00,22,00,00
,00,26,00,\

00,00,02,00,00,00,21,00,00,00,a0,0f,00,00,04,00,00,00,01,00,00,0
0,a0,0f,00,\
```

00,03,00,00,00,08,00,00,00,00,00,00,00

Dress Up Explorer Toolbar

Remember how nice IE3 once looked with a background image? Funny there is not one after IE4. Want to decorate your toolbar with a background image again? No problem. First, crank up the registry editor and navigate to HKEY_CURRENT_USER\SOFTWARE\Microsoft\ Internet Explorer\Toolbar\. Right-click in the right pane, add a New, String Value and name it "BackBitmap". Now right-click it, choose "Modify" and type in the path to a Bitmap image. Reboot, and your IE4 and Windows Explorer toolbars will be decorated. Make sure you choose a tiling bitmap image.

Customize Internet Explorer's Title Bar

Want to change IE's title caption as well? Open up the registry editor and scroll to HKEY_LOCAL_MACHINE\SOFTWARE\Microsoft\Internet Explorer\Main. Create a new string value on the right-pane named Window Title (note that there is a space between "Windows" and "Title" unlike OE which does not have a space in between). Change the value to the new name for the title caption. Restart to take effect.

Form AutoComplete

The first time you go to a webpage form with Internet Explorer and you enter some text in one of the form's boxes, the following dialogue box will come up.

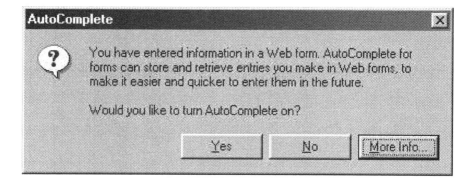

So how exactly can this speed up your working with forms?

1. Say, you have to type in a website address, However, in HTML form, the first time you enter <a href="http://www.activeie.com> Internet Explorer 5 will remember this. So the next time you go to the form page, you start to enter the same information you will get to about <a href="http://www.ac - and you can just use the down cursor to select the URL to auto complete. Check out the example below.

FTP Drag and Drop

Did you know that with Internet Explorer, you could now use the browser as your FTP client? Internet Explorer supports drag and drop FTP, Login etc, everything most FTP clients can do. Here is a simple tip on how to drag and drop FTP.

1. Open up Internet Explorer and load up any FTP site of your choice.

2. Next up: If you have gone to a FTP site in which you would like to download something then all you have to do is go into the folder the file is kept, and then DRAG the folder to your desktop or to any folder on your PC. Internet Explorer will then start to download it for you.

3. If you would like to upload a file to the FTP server, it is just as simple. Drag the file that you want to upload off your PC into Internet Explorer and watch it upload.

Disabling The Friendly http Error Messages

Internet Explorer recognizes http error messages (such as "Error 404: Page not found" etc.) and displays a friendly version in the browser. If you would prefer to see the proper error pages for the particular web server you are using, go to Tools, Internet Options and select the Advanced tab. Then uncheck the Show friendly http errors box.

Display Favorites

The interface itself is neat and tidy, and it is controlled from Favorites | Organize Favorites. He is where it all starts:

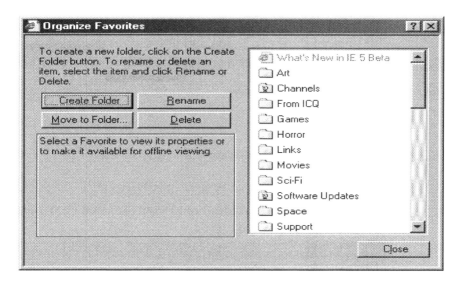

Here is a description of what they all mean:

• Create Folder - Clicking here is a pretty obvious one. This will create a new folder for you in your favorites.

• Delete - this option will either let you delete a whole folder, or simply delete a single favorite.

• Rename - this lets you rename any of your folders or single favorites.

• Move to Folder - Simply lets you move folders and favorites to different positions in the menu.

Now then, along the bottom of the menu are the newer options, here is what they do...Once you have selected a favorite or a folder that is.

• Make Available Offline - Synchronize means that Internet Explorer 5will download all of your favorites that you have selected to make sure you have the most up-to date information available to you.

145

Saving Favorites as a Webpage

With Internet Explorer 5, you can now export your favorites list to a .html page. This is useful for putting both a list of your favorite sites on your homepage, or to make use of Internet Explorer 5 favorites with Netscape Navigator. Read on and I will explain just how easy it is to do.

1. Open up Internet Explorer 5 and go to FILE | IMPORT/EXPORT.
2. Follow the instructions. Click on EXPORT.
3. Decide where you would like to save the list of favorites and then name it whatever you like.

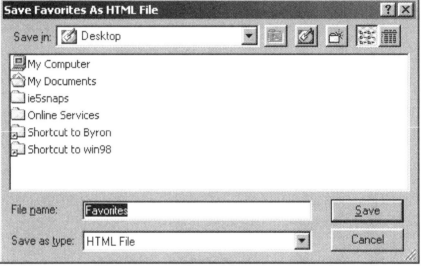

4. Now you will have a neat list of favorites in the form of a HTML document.

Remove The Favorites Folder From The Start Menu

Note: This is a registry edit.

146

"Go to:
Hkey_Current_User\Software\Microsoft\Windows\CurrentVersion
\Policies\Explorer
right click right pane and add the following new binary value:
"NoFavoritesMenu" and give it this hex value 01 00 00 00
Re-boot

This will get rid of the "Favorites" folder in the "Start" menu."

Synchronization

One of the new features of Internet Explorer 5 is Synchronization. This allows you to synchronize the contents of web sites on the Internet with those in your Offline Pages folder. With Synchronization, you can get Internet Explorer to ensure that you always have the most up-to-date pages to look at when you are working offline.

How to Synchronize

- When you find a Webpage that you like, in addition, you want to add it to your favorites list. Click FAVORITES | ADD TO FAVORITES and then click on MAKE AVAILABLE OFFLINE. Internet Explorer 5 will then proceed to download the website to your "OFFLINE PAGES" folder.

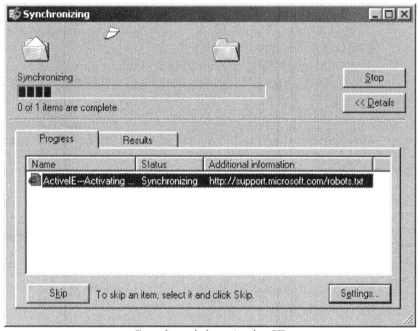

Synchronizing ActiveIE

Advanced Synchronizing

- Click on FAVORITES | ADD TO FAVORITES and MAKE AVAILABLE OFFLINE. Finally click on "CUSTOMIZE".

• This will bring up the "OFFLINE SYNCHRONIZATION WIZARD ". Click on NEXT.

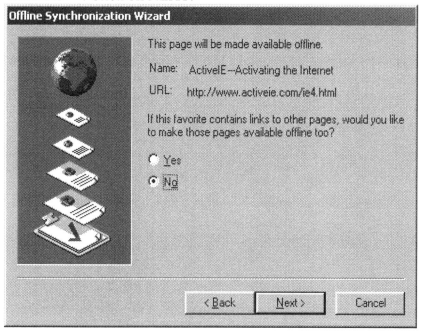

Decide if you would like to download the links that come off the webpage, you are synchronizing.

• The next list that comes up (Above) asks if you would like to make this favorite download the links that appear off the site in question. For this tip, click NO and then NEXT.

Set-up the times you wish to start Synchronizing.

• Finally, you have to decide at what times you would like Internet Explorer 5 to Synchronize your favorite. This I will leave for you to decide. It might be best for you to set-up the time to download the same for all pages you would like to Synchronize.

Importing and **Exporting**

Microsoft has tried to make it easier for you to move from one browser (Netscape) to another, there is a new Import and Export Wizard   accessed from the File/Import and Export... menu. The Wizard   has four options: Import Favorites, Export Favorites, Import Cookies, and Export Cookies. Choose one from the list and click the Next Button. You then choose to import or export from a specific application - compatible applications, like Netscape Communicator, will be listed in the drop down menu. Select this option by clicking on radio Button next to "Import from an application" (Assuming you have other applications that are supported) and then select the application from the drop down menu.

You can also choose a second option to import/export a specific file. This allows you to export your Favorites to a file (the default is one called bookmark.htm, which is the filename used by Navigator for storing its bookmarks - the equivalent of Favorites) on your drive. You can then, for example, give your bookmark file to another user who uses the Netscape browser on their machine. Likewise, cookies are exported to a file called cookie.txt, which is the filename used by Navigator. Obviously, the Import functions work in similarly, However, in reverse - you can import Favorites and Cookies from the application either directly or from a file.

Closing Parent Windows

If you are using multiple windows browsing, closing a whole bunch of parent windows will be annoying. No problem. Hold down the Shift key and close the child window. Bingo! All the parent windows will close automatically.

Opening New Window Under Single Window View

Users using single window browsing can easily open a new window by holding down Ctrl and then click on a folder.

Taking Over Window Under Multiple Window View

Like the tip above, users using multiple window browsing can easily force the new folder to open in the current window by holding down Ctrl and then click on a folder.

Deleting Without The Recycle Bin

To delete a file without going through the Recycle Bin, hold down Shift and delete.

Solving A Mouse Drag

If you have accidentally dragged an icon and wished you had not do it, the next time you come to this situation, hit the Esc key before you release the mouse Button. The icon will jump back to place.

Up One Level Key

Pressing the Backspace key under normal Windows or Explorer will bring you back to the parent folder, giving the same function as the "Up One Level" Button.

Switching Between Browsing & The Internet

Many of you might not notice this However, the Windows Explorer, and Internet Explorer has been bonded as one. The proof? The next time Windows Explorer comes up with and Illegal Operation error, all instances of Internet Explorer windows will close as well.

One of the coolest things to do with the Address Bar is, you can be browsing your folders and when you feel like it, type in an Internet URL, Dial-up Networking will appear and Windows Explorer will "morph" to Internet Explorer. Awesome! In addition, you will also find that browsing between folders and the Internet is fully supported by the Back and Next Button s. That means, if you opened Windows Explorer and then typed a URL and switched to IE, clicking on the Back Button will bring you back to Windows Explorer with the last folder you opened.

Because Windows Explorer and IE is one, the arrangement of your toolbars will also affect each other. How you arrange the toolbars under IE will look the same under Windows Explorer. The only difference is, if you are browsing through folders, windows will put up a "Windows" logo on the top right corner. When you switch to IE, the logo will change to the "IE" logo. That way, you will know where you are.

Online & Offline

On nice thing about the new IE is that it will notify you where you are. If you are browsing HTML files in your hard drive, Explorer will put a My Computer icon on the right side of the status bar. Go into a secure zone and a "lock" icon will appear. This is useful to know where you are. If you are using a HTML file in your hard drive using frames However, one of the frames are actually an online page, Explorer will notify you by placing a My Computer icon with the words "Mixed" beside it.

Browsing Files and the Internet Together

Okay, so the single Window options do not give you much flexibility when it comes to browsing folders and the Internet at the same time. So, try using Explorer instead. On the left pane of Explorer, click on the Internet Explorer. Hey, you now got the Internet inside Windows Explorer. To switch to real-time Internet Explorer mode, just close the All Folders toolbar. However, the toolbar itself has more tricks under its sleeve. Browsing the Internet with Windows Explorer gives you the option to navigate pages just like files on the left frame. This is better than the Back & Next Button s. Very useful for framed sites because it actually shows the file in the frames Useful is not it?

Open Folder With Explorer

Whenever you click on a folder shortcut on the desktop, a window will appear. If you want an Explorer-style view, right-click the folder shortcut and select Properties. Add the following line to the target text box before the folder path:

c:\windows\explorer.exe /n, /e,

For example, c:\windows\explorer.exe /n, /e, c:\games\ (we assume c:\games it the folder path). The next time you double-click this icon, Explorer will appear.

Browsing With The Address Bar

The URL bar is quite useful if you are willing to type fast instead of clicking on an endless list of folders. To turn this feature on, all you need to do is click on the View, Toolbar, and Address Bar. You can now move around with typing like DOS However, in Windows environment of course, Instead of just typing the folder path, you can actually launch programs by typing their full path just like the Run command. Note too that you can use the.. command to move up one level. For multiple levels, use the.../../ with each../ for a parent folder.

Search For Files With Auto-Complete

Looking for files under big folders like the C:\Windows\System\ folder can be quite a headache. However, it would be simpler if you have the Auto-Complete feature turned on. Type the first few letters and Windows will complete the filename with the best matching selection. Works better and more efficient than the Search option on single files.

Bypassing Useless Messages

By default, Windows will display an extra message for the Windows and System folders. This message will soon turn out to be annoying. To turn off this message, simply delete the folder.htt file in the directories and their gone.

Customizing Folders

Why not? The good thing about the new Explorer is it supports custom folders. Very useful is you have files on a folder that requires special attention. Click on the View | Customize this Folder... option. You can choose the options you prefer.

System Folder Views

 do not like the window view of My Computer, Recycle Bin, or the Control Panel? Customize them by searching for .http files at your C:\Windows\Web folder. They will contain appropriate names for you to find out.

Enabling Thumbnail View

If you have a directory just for storing images or HTML files like those that we do, you will find the preview Window on the left a very good help. However, to view them you must highlight them one by one. For a better option, right click any black space of the window and select Properties. Check the box Enable thumbnail view and click on OK. On the Explorer menu, click on View and you will find a new option - the Thumbnails view. The setting requires you to specify enable Thumbnails view on a folder-by-folder basis.

Pump Up Explorer View

We must admit that the folder view can pump up Explorer and do more advance options more than you can ever dream of. Ready to go? First, we must make sure we have a full view of everything. Go to the View, Folder Options menu. Click on the View tab. Make sure you have the Show all files option on. Next check Show me file attri However, es in Detail View. Apply these settings. Next, display this URL bar and status bar. Our advice is turn off the as web page view to speed things up a bit. Now, go detail view for optimum solution. Resize the panes to have a reasonable view. Great stuffs! Your Explorer is now pumped up and ready to go for more intense work.

Windows Explorer In Full Screen

The Full Screen option under Internet Explorer is such a favorite feature for most of us. It eliminates all unnecessary toolbars and gives you real-time full screen browsing. However, will not it be better if we can use Full Screen mode under Windows Explorer itself?

We have discussed how tightly the Windows Explorer and Internet Explorer are integrated. We all know very well that there is no Full Screen Button on Windows Explorer, or any folder window. However, there is an undocumented way to put Windows Explorer into full screen. First, we know that there is another way to activate the Full Screen mode - the F11 key. Now try it on explorer - hey, it just works! Press it again to restore it back to the Window mode. We realized that this do not just work on Windows Explorer, it would work on all folder windows.

All the Explorer Bars will slide off when you are not using the, under Full Screen mode. It stations them, press the pushpin Button. The full screen Explorer mode has proven to be rather useful if you are browsing a bit folder or you are using a low screen resolution.

Creating A Hidden Directory

It is amazing how useful this trick is. You have a private directory and you want it hidden to keep off snoopers. The Hidden attriHowever, e under Explorer is no use because people can use View Folder Options|View hidden files easily.

However, there is a solution to this. Go to MS DOS Prompt and type

MD names Alt+255

By holding down the Alt key, while typing 255 (numeric pad only) you will create a character that looks like an empty space. That means, your filename must not be more than 7 characters since Alt+255 already took up one. The next time anybody types the DIR command, they can see the directory However, to access it, you must type Alt+255 behind the filename. Without that, you will get an error message. With Windows Explorer, you cannot even open the directory because you will get a "Folder does not exist" error. So much for security!

Chapter 30

Windows 95/98 for Beginners

Converting to Fat32

If you upgraded to Windows 98 on an old system, odds are the disk uses the older 16-bit FAT, or file allocation table, instead of the newer 32-bit FAT. Windows 98 includes a conversion utility that updates your disk so you will not have to reformat it. To run the utility, choose Start|Programs|Accessories|System Tools|Drive Converter (FAT32), then work your way through the Drive Converter Wizard screens.

Note: There are some issues concerning the conversion to Fat32

Issues on converting to Fat32

Before you convert to FAT32, make sure it is the right choice for you. FAT32's strong point is that it uses hard disk space more efficiently. The minimum file size for FAT16 on a 1GB disk, for example, is 32K. For FAT32, it is 4K. Another benefit is that unlike FAT16, FAT32 is not limited to a 2GB-per-disk partition.

In addition, you cannot use DriveSpace to compress a FAT32 disk. And if you like to use your notebook's suspend-to-disk feature, it will not work with FAT32. Nor can you dual-boot your system to run earlier versions of Windows or DOS. Additionally, some older disk utilities work only with FAT16, so you may have to upgrade your third-party utility programs. And once you have converted to FAT32, the only way to return the disk to FAT16 and reclaim these capabilities is through repartitioning and reformatting.

If you choose to convert, the Drive Converter Wizard does a good job of warning you about possible problems. Be sure to read each screen carefully as you work your way through the choices, and do not hesitate to cancel the conversion if you have any doubts.

Note: Some drives you have may have bad sectors; if they do then you will have to format before running the Fat32 Converter.

Backup before converting to Fat32

If you are ready to convert your hard disk to FAT32, be sure to back up your data files beforehand addition;, preferably your entire disk--a good idea any time you are about to make significant changes to your hard disk. If you decide, you want to revert to FAT16--because you cannot live without your notebook's suspend-to-disk capability after all, for example--you will have to reformat the disk and reinstall everything from scratch, including Windows 98. If you have a backup, you can repartition, reformat, and then restore the disk instead of reinstalling individual programs. Ideally, you should use a backup program that includes a disaster-recovery feature, so you do not have to reinstall Windows before you run the restore.

Anti Virus software and **Fat32**

Converting a disk to FAT32 changes its partition table and boot record. If you are using antivirus software, it may intercept any attempt to update either or both and ask whether it is okay. Be sure to answer Yes. When you reboot your system after converting the disk, the antivirus software may notice the change and offer to fix it for you. Do not let it. If the software restores the partition table, the boot record, or both, you will not be able to access your hard disk or any data on it.

Stopping the conversion

After you run the FAT32 converter and reboot, Windows will automatically run Disk Defragmenter as part of the conversion procedure. This can take hours, so it is best to start the conversion when you know you will not need your computer for a while. If you need to use the computer, you can stop the defrag program in midstream and run it later. However, system performance may suffer until you restart the program and let it fully defrag the disk. To run Disk Defragmenter, choose Start|Programs|Accessories|System Tools|Disk Defragmenter, select the appropriate disk drive from the drop-down menu, and choose OK. Alternatively, you can go to My Computer, right-click the disk, and choose Properties|Tools|Defragment Now.

Basic Windows 95

Quick Access for Favorite Files. Save yourself time by creating a Shortcut to any document you load regularly. Simply right-drag the file onto your desktop and select Shortcut.

Desktop Floppy Access. For quicker access to your floppy drive, place a Shortcut on the desktop. In Explorer, My Computer, or any folder window, right-click the drive, drag it to the desktop, and when you let go, select Create Shortcut(s) Here.

Easy Move to Floppies. The Send To menu, which you can access by right-clicking a file and selecting Send To, lets you copy the file to drive A:. To move files there easily, use Notepad to create a text file called "Floppy move.bat," with the line @ move %1 a:, in the c:\windows\sendto folder.

Name That Tune. If your old CD-ROM drive does not play audio CDs automatically, you can at least make it play them semi automatically. Right-click the desktop and select New *Shortcut. Enter the commandline c:\windows\cdplayer.exe /play. Click Next, name the Shortcut, and click Finished. Now all you need to do is pop in a CD and double-click the Shortcut.

Making a Good Pointer. Want to have some fun with your mouse cursors? Select Start*Control Panel, double-click Mouse, and go to the Pointers page. Highlight the pointer you would like to change, click Browse, and double-click a pointer you want to change to. Select Apply or OK to make your change stick.

Folder Jumping. "Times New Roman" Would you rather type than click? In Explorer, you can jump to any folder or file by typing the first few letters of its name very quickly. Just do not type too slowly, or Windows will jump to a file whose name begins with the second letter you type.

Does <Caps Lock> Ring a Bell? Have you ever hit the <Caps Lock>, <Scroll Lock>, or <Num Lock> key by mistake? To make those keys sound a warning tone when they are tapped, go to Control Panel, double-click Accessibility Options, select Use ToggelKeys, and click OK.

Finders, Keepers. If you use Windows Find to search for the same set of files regularly--for instance, to locate all the files in c:\data saved in the last month--you can save your search criteria for later use. After you have clicked Find Now and you have your results, select File*Save Search. Windows will create on the desktop a Shortcut to that exact find.

Explorer View, Please. Switching an open folder to an Explorer view is an easy and efficient way to browse from folder to folder. To open an Explorer view, right-click the icon in the upper left corner of the window and chooses Explore.

The Captain's Log. You can use Notepad to create a time-stamped log file-and y tool for logging your voice mail or creating a to-do list. Simply type .LOG as the only text in the first line of a Notepad file. Then make your entries, save the file, and close it. Next time you open the file, you will see that Notepad has added a time-in addition;-date stamp beneath each entry.

Long File Name Compatibility. Windows 3.x applications generally work fine with Win 95's long file names; not so, with utilities, which can truncate long names. If the documentation does not explicitly say the utility is compatible with Windows 95, do not use it.

Long File Names No Longer. Some old, obscure DOS programs can wipe out a file's long name. If you must keep such a program, disable long file names. Right-click My Computer and select Properties, then Performance. Click the File System Button and select the Troubleshooting tab. Check Disable long name preservation for old programs and click OK.

Emergency Startups. If you cannot boot your hard drive, you will be glad you have a start-up floppy disk and y. To create one, from Control Panel double-click Add/Remove Programs. Insert your disk, select the Startup Disk tab, and click Create Disk.

FAT32 and Defrag Don'ts. do not defragment a FAT32 partition with anything However, a defragged that supports FAT32. The one that came with your computer, which you will find at Start*Programs* Accessories*System Tools*Disk Defragmenter, will do fine.

How Hard Is Your CPU Working? If you have changed your system's configuration, you can use System Monitor to see the effect of those changes on performance. You can measure the difference in performance between two hard drives to determine if the upgrade was worth it. From the Start menu, select Programs*Accessories*System Tools*System Monitor.

If System Monitor is not there, you will need to install it. Put your Windows 95 disc in your CD-ROM drive. When the blue Windows 95 window comes up, click Add/Remove Programs. Click the Windows Setup tab, double-click Accessories, check System Monitor, and click OK twice.

Display for Yourself. do not want other folks messing with your wallpaper or screen resolution? The Windows 95 System Policy Editor is great for restricting access to your Display Properties dialog box. Select File*Open Registry, double-click the Local User icon, double-click Control Panel, and then open the Display book. Select Restrict Display Control Panel and take your pick of options at the bottom of the dialog box--for example, use Disable Display Control Panel to keep people out altogether. Save your changes and exit.

In addition's Off My Registry. Playing with the Registry is an invitation to disaster, and the Windows 95 System Policy Editor can keep people out of it. To lock people out of your Registry, select File*Open Registry, double-click the Local User icon, and double-click System and then Restrictions. Select Disable Registry Editing Tools. Save your changes and exit.

Conceal Your Entire Past. To erase the Start menu's Documents list entirely, at least until you next create or save a file, right-click an empty spot on the Taskbar, select Properties, click the Start Menu Programs tab, click Clear, and then click OK.

Longest Battery Life. You can conserve battery power on a notebook PC by setting Windows 95 to do a minimal amount of disk caching. Right-click My Computer and select Properties. From the Performance tab, click File System. On the Hard Disk tab, make sure Mobile or docking system is selected under 'Typical role of this machine'. Your system will not be as fast as it was before, However, it will last longer on a battery charge.

Explorer less File Management. You can manage files right inside your applications. The Save As and Open dialog boxes of Windows 95-savvy applications offer full drag-and-drop capabilities and the same right-click menu you get in Explorer or a stand port folder window.

Seven Megabytes Richer. Looking to free up some disk space? Check your Windows\Help folder for AVI files--you could have as much as 7MB of them left over from Windows' tutorial. Unless you are using Windows 95 for the first time, you do not need them.

Good Storage With ClipBook. There is some amazing, little-known stuff on the Windows 95 CD-ROM--for instance, a better version of Clipboard. When you copy or cut something to the usual Clipboard, you lose the last thing that was there. Few people know it, However, Windows 95 also has a ClipBook where you can save clippings and reuse them. To install it, insert the Windows 95 CD-ROM, and in the resulting window select Add/Remove Software. Go to the Windows Setup tab, click Have Disk, click Browse, and navigate your way to d:\Other\Clipbook (where d is your CD-ROM drive letter). With the clipbook.inf file the only thing in the file name box, click OK twice. Check ClipBook Viewer, then click

Install. You will now be able to open the program by selecting Start*Programs*Accessories*ClipBook Viewer.

Back Up Your Registry. All sorts of installation programs mess with the Windows Registry, so it is a good idea to make regular backup copies of the two files, user.dat, and system.dat. Unfortunately, you cannot use Explorer or DOS to copy these files.

Buried on the Windows 95 installation CD-ROM is a program that lets you make up to nine backups of your Registry. Just copy Cfgback.exe from the CD-ROM's \Other\Misc\Cfgback folder to c:\windows, and then copy the Cfgback.hlp file to c:\windows\help. To make a backup, double-click Cfgback.exe and follow the detailed instructions.

Keep Policy Editor Off Your Hard Drive. do not want someone else changing your Windows environment? Use the System Policy Editor, located on the Win 95 installation CD-ROM. do not put the Policy Editor on your own hard drive or you will make it too easy for others to change your configuration. When you need it, pop in the CD-ROM, select Start*Run, and run the commandd:\admin\apptools\poledit\poledit.exe, where d is your CD-ROM drive.

Windows 95 Resource Kit. If you need the inside scoop on Win 95's import s, take a look at the Windows 95 Resource Kit, hidden on the installation CD-ROM. There you will find information on everything from configuring a dial-up server to how device drivers work. To read this help file, place the CD-ROM in your drive, browse to the d:\admin\reskit\helpfile folder (where d is your CD-ROM drive letter), and double-click win95rk.hlp. To make the Resource Kit a permanent part of your hard drive, copy win95rk.hlp and win95rk.cnt to your c:\windows\help folder, then create a Shortcut to win95rk.hlp.

Enhanced Printer Troubleshooter. Having trouble with your printer? The Windows 95 installation CD-ROM contains a printer-troubleshooting program that may be able to help. Place the CD-ROM in your drive, browse to the d:\other\misc\epts folder (where d is your CD-ROM drive letter), and double-click epts.exe. The program will ask you what kind of problem you are having, then continue to ask questions and offer solutions until you solve your problem or give up.

The Windows 98 Disk Cleanup tool that is built into Windows 98 can help you free up space. Disk Cleanup starts automatically under certain conditions--for example, if you copy a file to a hard disk with less than 3% free space, say, 30MB on a 1GB hard disk. However, it is a good idea to use the program regularly, so you do not reach that 3% threshold in the first place.

To start the utility, choose Start|Programs|Accessories|System Tools|Disk Cleanup. The program opens a dialog with two tabs: Disk Cleanup and More Options. The Disk Cleanup tab includes a Files to remove list box; there are four basic check-box items--Temporary Internet Files, Downloaded Program Files, Recycle Bin, and Temporary files--though you may see others (for details, see the next tip). Choose More Options, and you will see two choices--Windows setup and Installed programs--, which you also can access through the Control Panel's Add/Remove Programs option. These let you remove unneeded Windows components or application programs. If your disk does not use the FAT32 file system, you will also see an option for converting it to FAT32.

SYMPTOMS ERROR MESSAGE ON A BLUE SCREEN

When you start Windows, you may receive the following error message on a blue screen:
WINDOWS This program has caused a Fatal Exception 0D at 00457:000040B1 and will be terminated.
Pressing any key causes, the screen to turn black and the computer to stop responding (hang).

CAUSE

This error message can occur if you are using Adobe Type Manager with certain video adapter drivers and the Hardware Acceleration setting is not set to Full.

RESOLUTION

To resolve this issue, set the Hardware Acceleration setting to Full. To do so, follow these steps:

1. Restart your computer in Safe mode. To do so:
- Windows 95:

Restart your computer. When you see the "Starting Windows 95" message, press the F8 key, and then choose Safe Mode from the Startup menu.
Windows 98:

Restart your computer, press and hold down the CTRL key after your computer completes the Power On Self Test (POST), and then choose Safe Mode from the Startup menu.

2. Click Start, point to Settings, and then click Control Panel.
3. Double-click System.
4. Click the Performance tab, and then click Graphics.
5. Move the Hardware Acceleration slider all the way to the right (to the Full setting), and then click OK.
6. Click OK. When you are prompted to restart your computer, click Yes.

SYMPTOMS

When you start Windows 98, you do not see a "Starting Windows 98" message, and you cannot tell when to press the CTRL key to display the Windows 98 Startup menu.

CAUSE

The prompt has been removed to allow for a faster start of Windows 98.

RESOLUTION

To display the Startup menu, press and hold down the CTRL key when your computer starts.

NOTE: If you press and hold down the CTRL key when your computer starts, you may receive a Keyboard error message. If this occurs, you may safely ignore the Keyboard error message.

STATUS

This behavior is by design.

MORE INFORMATION

If you want the Windows 98 Startup menu to appear each time you start your computer, follow these steps:

1. Click Start, click Run, type the following command in the Open box, and then press ENTER:

msconfig
2. Click Advanced on the General tab, and then click the Enable Startup Menu check box to select it.
3. Click OK, click OK, and then click Yes.

Back To File & Program Manager

It is weird why some people still insist on sticking back to the "good old days" and still prefer to use File Manager and Program Manager over Explorer. If you still want to use them, open the Run menu and type *winfile.exe* for File Manager and *progman.exe* for Program Manager. If you still want another old friend back, try the Task Manager. Type *taskman.exe* for at the Run menu.

Details On Selecting Icons

Windows 3.1 comes with the click-to-select and double-click-to-launch system. Windows 95 refines this. It has an enhancement over Windows 3.1 - a better icon selection system. To select more than one icon, hold down the Ctrl key to select highlight another icon. To select all However, a few icons, hold down Ctrl+a to select all icons and use the Ctrl key to deselect the ones you do not want. The more convenient way is to hold down the Shift key, click on one icon and then on another icon and all the icons in between the 2 icons you selected will be highlighted as well.

Another nifty trick is the "lasso" technique. Hold down you left mouse Button and drag along - you will see that all icons in the area you dragged will be highlighted. The right-drag will work as a lasso too. The use of a right-drag, a menu will appear and if you can view the size of files or change the attriHowever, es to a bunch of files quickly under Properties.

Windows 3.1 allows you to type the first character of the word and Windows will hunt the icon with the best matching first character. No doubts that there will be a lot of icons with the same first character. Windows 95 improves this and you can now type the second, third even fourth character after the first matching one, if you can type that fast. Chances are, after the third matching character, Explorer probably already got the icon right.

Windows 98 users will have a more different interface However, it is mostly the same with just that they use point to highlight icons and single click to activate them.

Associating & Re-associating Files

If you have once opened an unknown file, Windows will prompt you to open that file with another program. If you like to always, open that file under that program, check Always use this program to open this type of file and Windows will do that. However, if you would like to manually take control over your files instead of Windows prompting you when needed, there is a way. Open Windows Explorer. Click on the View menu and select Folder Options. Next, click on the File Types tab. Double-click the file you want to associate. Double-click on the Open command. Type the full path of the new application to open it. Close all windows.

A simpler way to do this is to hold down Shift and double-click the file. There will be a new Open with command. Select your new application to open the file.

Make Use Of The Links Toolbar

Ever wondered why Windows is including the Links bar into Explorer? Basically, not all of us use the links bar. It is just sitting on Internet Explorer and usually achieves nothing. We usually just disable it.

Well, actually, there is a way to make use of this. You will find that the Links Bar works with Windows Explorer. The thing is, it can be used to benefit you. First, to organize this. There is no way to customize this through the toolbar itself. Click on the Favorites and select Organize Favorites. Select the Links folder. Now for some major editing.

You will find that the icons in the Links toolbar has too many text. This will take up lots of space. Rename the icons (through the Favorites menu) to a shorter name. Now, if you want to use this toolbar under Windows Explorer, make sure it suits Windows Explorer. Just a few weblinks would do - leave the rest at the Favorites menu. Add a Show Desktop icon or a link to My Computer and Control Panel. A link to a few of your most often accessed folder would also be fine.

If you want to use a lot of icons, give them short names and differentiate them with custom icons. Right-click the shortcut, select Properties and on the Shortcut tab, click on Change Icons. The rest is self-explanatory.

Scandisk Tips

Almost nothing has changed in the Windows 98 version of Scandisk; However, there is at least one potentially critical difference. If you turn off or reboot your system without going through the Shut Down procedure, Scandisk will not only run automatically the next time you boot up--the same as it does in Windows 95 OSR2--However, it will run without stopping (unless you stop it) or waiting for your input. This means you can use Windows 98 for applications such as unattended communications using a remote-operations program like Carbon Copy or PC Anywhere. If the system shuts down for any reason--because of a momentary power failure, for example--it will reboot without waiting for the okay to run Scandisk. If you are at your computer when it reboots, you can skip Scandisk, if you prefer. Simply choose the Exit Button on the Scandisk screen.

Clearing The Documents Menu

A super big Documents menu is not very much appreciated especially when you have to scroll for ages to get it. Go to your C:\Windows\recent folder. You will find all your recent documents there. Feel free to delete. Rest assures that they are only shortcuts and will not delete the file itself.

Decoding - New Scandisk option

One other change you will notice is a new choice in the Advanced Options dialog box. To run Scandisk manually, choose Start|Programs|Accessories|System Tools|Scandisk, and then choose the Advanced Button to view the advanced options. The one new choice is the less-than-self-explanatory "Report MS-DOS mode name length errors." This refers to the 8.3-format filename you will see if you are in DOS mode or a DOS window. Win 95 and Win 98 save each filename in both a long format and the 8.3 format. This option tells Scandisk to check the 8.3-format version of the name.

Find Out What You are Deleting

Before you delete files with Disk Cleanup, make sure you know exactly what you are deleting. The first two items you will find in the "Files to remove list" are Temporary Internet Files and Downloaded Program Files, both of which refer to directories that Internet Explorer 4 uses for files it downloads to your hard disk.

If you delete these files, you will just end up downloading them again the next time you visit the Web pages; if the pages are on your hard disk, however, they will load more quickly. If you clean out these directories too often--say, weekly--you will waste time downloading the same pages over and over. The Files to remove list shows how much disk space you will reclaim by deleting each item. If you will gain only a few megabytes by selecting these two choices, you may want to uncheck the boxes.

The third choice on the Files to remove list is Recycle Bin; checking it will empty it. The Temporary files option lets you delete files that various programs have put on your disk. These are usually safe to delete.

Next up is "Temporary Files". These are the files that are kept in you are, Windows/Temp folder that are generally of no use at all. These are also usually safe to delete.

Finally, we have "Delete Windows 98 uninstall information". This tends to be about 50-70 MB's of information. If you decide to delete this, then you must understand that you cannot go back to your former version of Windows without completely reinstalling.

View The List Of Files To Delete

If you have any doubts about which items you can safely tell Disk Cleanup to delete, most of the items under Files to remove give you a list of proposed deletions. Simply select an item and choose the View Files Button. The Button will disappear if you select Temporary files, presumably to prevent you from manually deleting a temporary file that a program is using.

While you are viewing these lists, you can delete files manually by selecting them and choosing File|Delete. With the Recycle Bin, for example, you might want to click the Date Deleted Button to sort the list by date and look at the most recently deleted files. (Recent deletions are the ones you are most likely to discover you need after all.) If you see, any that you want to keep, select all the others manually, and delete them with the File|Delete command.

Internet Shortcuts

You know of a way to create a shortcut to a site without adding it to the Favorites list that is, drag the entire document, and drop it on the desktop. Windows will create a shortcut there for you. However, it is not totally necessary to do that just to add a link to a website.

Create a new shortcut. Under the commandline, type in the URL of a website such as http://www.activewin.com. Then, give it the name, ActiveWindows. The next time you click on the shortcut, it will bring you here to us!

Mail Shortcuts

The above trick has been known by most of you. Here is another good However, less known one. Create a new shortcut. Under the commandline, type in mailto:askus@activewin.com. Give it an appropriate name such as Ask ActiveWindows. Now, the next time you click on the mail link, your e-mail program will launch and you will have a mail - with the e-mail address already typed, ready to be sent.

Now that was pretty cool, However, there is more! If you want to send mail to more than just one recipient, type in mailto:askus@activeie.com;wayne@activeie.com. Instead of just sending the mail to one person, you will now be sending it to 2 people. However, still some of you ask how to pre-set the subject of the mail as well. Just like HTML mailtos, type in mailto:askus@activewin.com?subject=PC Problems. Quite simple is not it?

In addition, you can also use carbon copy: mailto:askus@activewin.com?cc=wayne@activeie.com or blind carbon copy: mailto:askus@activewin.com?bcc=wayne@activeie.com. Here is something to really interest you. You can define the body or contents of the mail itself other than just the subject and recipients like this: mailto:askus@activewin.com?body=I have a slight problem here

Remember we said we do not know a way to link up more than 2 attriHowever, es at one time? Well now, you can! You will need the "&" character like this: mailto:askus@activewin.com?subject=PC Problems &cc=wayne@activeie.com&body=Body.

The only drawback here is like any other shortcuts; you are only allowed 255 characters in the commandline. Use them wisely.

Removing Control Panel Applets

Yeah, the Control Panel is considered as every Windows 98 user's friend. However, some certain applications comes with their own Control Panel applet. Sure, why not? It can be useful such as the DirectX, TweakUI, or Music controls bundled by your sound card. However, if you find the Control Panel crowded, you cannot just right-click the item and delete. However, you can remove it in a sneaky way.

Go to your C:\Windows\System\ directory and use the Search tool to search for *.cpl files. These files are the Control Panel applets or files. Since the names are not so organized, check which applet you want to remove, press delete or move them to another folder and they are off your Control Panel for good.

Channel Bar

Windows 98 comes with a "desktop" component called the Channel Bar. There will always be few channels pre-installed in your Channel Bar depending on the location of your country and the company, which you got your Windows 98 from. All your subscriptions to the Active Channels are stored here.

A channel is actually a website pushed to deliver information right on your desktop. To view a channel select it in the Channel Bar, or select a category, then select a channel inside. In the resulting window, click the Add Active Channel link, and you will see a dialog box asking if you would like to subscribe to the channel.

If you would like Internet Explorer to notify you of channel updates & download channel content on a regular basis for viewing offline, select the third option: Yes, Notify Me Of Updates And Download the Channel for Offline Viewing. Click the Customize Button , complete the options in the resulting dialog boxes--how much of the channel you would like to download, whether you want to be notified of updates via e-mail, and the subscription update schedule--clicking Next after each; then click Finish. Click OK, and your subscription is a done.

Managing The Channel Bar

After finding it useful, you will also find that the Channel Bar can sometimes be a pain too. Those channels will start to pile up and crowd your Channel Bar. You will have to scroll more and more to reach the bottom of the list. Worse still, there are still some sub-channels to hide inside main categories. Some of these can reach 100 channels!

It is time for a little housekeeping work. Deleting channels is so simple. Just right-click the channel, select Delete and it is gone. To add, just click on the View Channels Button on the taskbar (assuming you have the Quick Launch Button) and from the menu, and preview the channels. After being satisfied with the channels, click on the Add Active Channel link to subscribe it. Select subscription type and you are done.

Creating Desktop Shortcuts Without The Desktop Being In View

From a Windows Explorer or the normal My Computer window, for example, simply right-click the filename for which you want to create a Shortcut and choose Send To|Desktop As Shortcut. Everything else is then done for you. You can then rename the shortcut later if it is necessary.

Using Scrap Files

With my last tip, I taught you how to create a shortcut to a document. On this one, I will teach you how to save a portion of selected text. Again, this tip will not with all word processors.

In Word or WordPad, highlight a block of text. Drag it to the desktop. Windows will create this block of text as a Scrap file. Do not underestimate the use of scrap files. Imagine you have 3-5 lines or quotes which you want to keep repeating on several pages. The Copy-Paste will not work so well with multiple selections.

All you need to do is to copy out the "scraps" into the desktop before and with appropriate names. Resize your word processor nicely so that part of it can show the desktop. When you need a selected block of text, just drag it into the word processor.

Hiding The My Computer Icon

If you find the My Computer icon a pest and you want to remove it, there is actually no way to remove it. There is a registry hack, which we do not recommend at all. OK, let us make it a deal. If we cannot remove it, why not try our best to hide it? At least it is a better than none.

First of all, we need to create a an "invisible" icon. Go to my icon-creating guide. Just make the whole image blank. Now, right-click the desktop and select Properties. Click on the Effects tab (or the Plus! tab if you are using Windows 95 with Plus! installed). Point the icon path to the blank icon. Apply changes and now you have a blank My Computer icon.

Now for the next problem - the name. Windows will not accept blank space as a full filename. We need a filename that looks like an empty space However; it is not to trick Windows. Hold down your Alt and type 0160 on the numeric keypad.

Now we have a invisible My Computer icon. The final step - to keep it out of reach. Put it in a place where you will never click at all. Put it on maybe the edge of the desktop or somewhere better.

Maximize, Minimize & Close All Windows

This is common. You have a handful of applications, which you want to close. Surely you do not close each Window one by one? Hold down the Ctrl key and click on the application you want to close on the taskbar. Right-click one of them. There will be a context menu for you to Close, Minimize or Maximize. Select one action and all the applications you selected will close, minimize or maximize at the same time!

Secrets To A More Beautiful Desktop

OK - a beautiful desktop is not just for couch potatoes. A nice desktop can sometimes affect your working mood. We have a couple of tips to help your desktop stay forever "beautiful & young".

Get A Nice Wallpaper

"Sure", you say. Who does not have a good wallpaper? You have Plus! and all the wallpapers are cool enough. If you like cartoons, Plus98! themes should keep you contented. However, if you want some awesome and stunning artwork, you have not seen anything yet. We found out that some art gallery sites such as http://download.com.com/3150-2049-0.html?tag=dir , offers breath-taking 3D rendered artworks for wallpapers. I guarantee once you get a few of them on your desktop, you will not want to switch back to your old wallpapers ever again.

Remember that a nice wallpaper can eat up to a gigantic 3-5 megabytes. This will consume a lot of system resources. If you have a graphic conversion program, convert it to JPEG or GIF. This will compress up to 10 times the original size and will not suffer quality loss.

Less Clutter, More Space (And Speed Too!)

A very cluttered desktop makes things hard to find and might even cloud a beautiful wallpaper. Our advice - only the most important icons should stay on the desktop. The rest must go. In addition, also remember that the less active desktop components are there, the better because they can cause the desktop to be complicated and slow. You will find that a clean desktop will look very neat and the refresh and startup-loading rate will be much faster because there are fewer items now.

do not let Icons Get In The Way

Icons are just companions to the desktop. do not let icons effect the desktop. As we said, if you want to preserve the beauty of a wallpaper and you think icons are getting in the way, use my icon creating guide to create a transparent icon. The using the Display Properties, set My Computer, Network Neighborhood and Recycle Bin to the same transparent icon. Change the Desktop text to suit the wallpaper. That way, only the text will show up and blend nicely with the wallpaper.

More Multimedia On The Desktop

If you are quite experienced in HTML, DHTML or some programming code However, never put them into good use, now is the time to show them off. You can add ActiveX pop-up menus, HTML hyperlinks, maybe a song list, or anything that your imagination can think of However, it will be in a HTML file. Note that you must enable your desktop as webpage to display HTML files.

Tip: do not think that your wallpaper will have to go if you use HTML files - you can still display them by using them as a HTML file background image.

If You do not need It, do not use It

If you do not need the active desktop, you cannot disable your desktop as web page. All you need to do is to right-click the desktop, select Active Desktop and check off View as Web page. You will find that it will speed up the desktop dramatically.

Deleting Subscriptions

Just subscribe to a channel However, now feel like not liking it now? do not worry; you can delete any subscription easily. In any open Explorer window, select Favorites, Manage Subscriptions. In the Subscriptions window, right-mouse-click the subscription you want to delete and select Delete. Click Yes to confirm, and that subscription is history.

Modifying Subscriptions

If you are not satisfied with a subscription's settings, you can always change that as well. In an open Explorer window, select Favorites, Manage Subscriptions. In the Subscriptions window, right-mouse-click the subscription you want to change and selects Properties. Select the Receiving tab to change the subscription type and e-mail notification options. Select the Schedule tab to change the update schedule. Complete any changes, click OK, and the new settings take effect immediately.

Rearranging Your Channels

Done with the trimming part? Now, it is time to start rearranging the channels. For example, you might like to move some of the visible channels away inside one of the channel categories listed at the top of the bar. Or you might want to arrange the list according to the frequency of use.

Like all Windows/Internet Explorer stuff, channels can also be dragged and dropped. A gray vertical line will appear between the channels when your mouse hovers a place, which is suitable. Drop the channel and let them slide up or down themselves.

To move a channel into a channel category, select that category to open its window, and then move your mouse pointer to the left edge of your screen to make the Channel Bar appear. Click and drag a channel from the Channel Bar into the blank space in the open window, let go, and that channel joins the ranks of the others in that category. Just the opposite, you can move a channel from an open category to the "main" Channel Bar.

And if you want to uncluttered the Channel Bar However, are still afraid that you might want to use some of them some other time, the solution is simple. Drag the channel from the Channel Bar to the desktop. It will stay on the desktop and be removed from the Channel Bar. To restore channel, simply drag it back to the Channel Bar again. It is better that you create a folder just to store unneeded channels for future use.

Creating Document Shortcuts

With some programs, like Word, you can create a Shortcut by selecting a block of text, right clicking the selection, and dragging it to the desktop. When you release the Button, Windows opens a menu. Choose the option Create Document Shortcut Here. When you are ready to work with the file again, choose the Shortcut. Windows does not only launch the program for you and load the document; it will also return you to the passage you originally selected when you created the Shortcut. It even highlight's the text to make it even easier for you to get straight back to work.

Note: Not all word processors that are available support this feature.

Using An HTML Document As Desktop Wallpaper

One of the greatest things about the Active Desktop is that it lets you have a HTML page as your desktop wallpaper. In addition, you can take advantage of any links defined in the document. Click on a URL in the wallpaper, for example, and Windows calls up Internet Explorer and connects to that address.

To use this feature, first create the document and move it to the Windows\Web\Wallpaper directory or wherever you choose. Then right-click the desktop and choose Properties to open the Display Properties dialog box, with the Background tab showing. If you put the file in the Wallpaper directory, Windows will list it in the text box labeled "Select An HTML Document Or Picture." If you put it elsewhere, choose the Browse Button to find it. Select the file and choose OK. If you do not have the Active Desktop enabled, Windows will ask if you want to enable it. Answer Yes. That is all there is to it. Windows will now use the document as your desktop background.

Using A Website Page As Desktop Wallpaper

You can also download a Web page to use as wallpaper. Go to the Web page of your choice using Internet Explorer and choose File|Save As. Navigate to the directory you want to save the file in (preferably Windows\Web\Wallpaper), enter a filename, and choose Save. Then follow the instructions above, and the Web page will display as your desktop background.

Adding AVI Wallpaper

Add live, seamless video directly to your desktop using Microsoft Word. First, you will need a free Word add-on called Internet Assistant for Microsoft Word an .AVI file to display, in addition;, of course, Internet Explorer 4.0 (or Memphis). After installing Internet Assistant, open notepad and save the blank file as VIDEO.HTM. Open Word, and then open the new VIDEO.HTM file. Select Picture from the Insert menu and select the "Video" tab.

Use the browse Button to select your .AVI file. Click OK and close Word. Right-click on the desktop, select Properties and click on the "Desktop" tab. Click on the "New" Button, select "Web site" and click OK. Use the browse Button to find VIDEO.HTM. Click OK, then OK again. Now you have a live video on your desktop you can resize and move.

WinKey Shortcuts

Other than just bringing up the start menu, the WinKey has other special functions.

WinKey+E	Open an Explorer window
WinKey+R	Open the Run dialog
WinKey+Pause	Open the System Properties
WinKey+F	Find: All Files
WinKey+Ctrl+	Find: Computer
WinKey+M	Minimize all open windows
WinKey+D	Show/Hide Desktop
WinKey+Shift	Undo minimize all open windows
WinKey+Tab	Cycle through taskbar program Button s
WinKey+F1	Open Windows Help

Using HotKeys On The Desktop

This is a terrific tip a lot of people overlooked. You can actually assign hotkeys for all your shortcuts on your desktop. Right-click the desktop shortcut and select Properties. Click on the Shortcut tab. In the Shortcut key text box, choose what the combination of shortcut key you want is. Hold down Ctrl+Alt or Ctrl+Shift combination while selecting another key.

Assigning custom hotkeys to shortcuts

We realized that you could even activate the hotkey without the desktop in view! However, you have to make sure your hotkey combination will not clash with the key commands of the active application.

Taskbar & Start Menu

Hiding Start Menu Folders

It is surprisingly easy how you want the some certain folders in the start menu (the StartUp menu for example) hidden up nicely. All you need to do is to right-click the StartUp folder on the start menu. Right-click it and when a pop-up menu appears, choose Properties. Change the attriHowever, e to hidden. Since the start-menu will not display hidden items, it will not be displayed.

This is very useful when you want to unclutter the start menu temporarily and do not want to remove them. To restore them? No problem, just open the C:\Windows\Start Menu folder (or right-click the start Button and select Open) and change the attriHowever, es again.

Using The URL Address Bar

First things first, you may not have the address bar on your taskbar when you first install Windows 98. To make sure it is set-up Right click on your taskbar and then move to Toolbars and then check Address.

The Address toolbar is a text box that works like the URL address box in a Web browser like Internet Explorer. When you enter a URL (or an HTML filename with drive and path), Windows passes the information to your default browser, which connects to the Internet, if necessary, and goes to the appropriate address or file. You can also click the arrow to the right of the text box for a drop-down list of recently used addresses.

You cannot drag filenames or Shortcuts to the Address toolbar to create new Shortcuts, However, you can quickly open a Web page by choosing Start|Run, then typing a URL or HTML filename in the Open text box, which includes a drop-down list of most recently used entries. If you prefer the Keyboard to the mouse, you will probably prefer the Start|Run command, because you will not have to take your hands off the Keyboard .

Adding Shortcuts To Your Start Menu

You can drag and drop to insert a Shortcut in a Start menu submenu very easily. To place a Shortcut in your Programs group, for example, drag the filename to the Start Button, hover over it until the Start menu opens, then drag the filename to your Programs menu and hover over it until the Programs menu opens. You can then drag the Shortcut to any spot on the Programs menu or hover over one of the third-level menu items to open it and then drag the Shortcut there. Again, as you drag the Shortcut, Windows inserts a divider to indicate the Shortcut's position.

Moving Shortcuts Around

Windows will automatically place shortcuts in alphabetical order. If you have a program you use more frequently, just drag it to the top of the order as shown above. Now, we all know we can add items to the start menu as first-level items. However, all items will be placed above the Programs menu separated with a divider. You can actually drag an item between the Run and Programs menu and it will stay there!

Working With Toolbars

Toolbars are probably one of the most useful features in IE4 / Windows 98. It helps unclutter too many items on both the Start Menu and Desktop. Furthermore, it supports autohide. We will show you how to improve your computing environments with these toolbars.

Choosing Toolbars

By default, Windows will come with the Quick Launch toolbar installed. The most useful Button is perhaps the "Show Desktop" Button. Click on it to show the desktop. Click again to switch back to your applications. To create toolbars, all your need to do is to right-click any empty space of the taskbar, select Toolbars, and select any toolbars you want.

Managing Toolbars

All the items in the toolbars are manageable. Right-click on Button s to rename, copy, cut, delete and view properties. Next, to change the appearance of the toolbar, right-click on the toolbar and you can decide whether you want large icons or small icons, show or hide titles or show or hide text.

Custom Toolbars

You can create any toolbar by right clicking the taskbar, select Toolbars, New Toolbar... and select folder. The contents of the folder will be displayed as Button s. The catch? The toolbar becomes the real thing - if you delete or add items to the toolbar, it will be removed or added into the folder itself. Great of you want to manage your folders from the taskbar. Else, you will find this a big annoyance. The solution out is to create a folder just for toolbars. Dump just shortcuts into it and you no longer have to worry about messing up your original files.

Slide & Stack

If you have a bunch of toolbar, you will notice that you can actually stack toolbars on top of each other to save space. A small arrow will appear for you to scroll the toolbar from end to end. Great However, if you want to have a full view of it, resizing it time and again is not in your computing wish list. Worry not. Just double-click on any toolbar and they will slide to full view. The best way is to enable the "Show Title" option and size it until only the title is in view. Now, whenever you need it, just double-click it to slide out and double-click again to slide back. The drawback here is that all other toolbars in front of the sliding toolbar will slide with it. When you slide that toolbar back, the other moved toolbars however will not slide back with it. So, try to make the more frequent sliding toolbar towards s the left side to prevent from moving other toolbars as well.

Out Of The Taskbar

Toolbars do not have to stick to the taskbar. They can be independent toolbars on the desktop. Just create a toolbar and then drag it to the side of the desktop. It will be something like the taskbar itself However, only just Button s. Right-click and select Auto Hide and Always On Top and you have a power-toolbar even that will appear when the desktop is out of sight or IE in full screen. Your do not have to worry about the toolbar popping out at wrong time because you will have to go to the very edge of the screen to do that. Try having toolbars at all 3 sides (excluding the taskbar of course).

Floating Toolbars

If you run out of space for your toolbars and you have a uncluttered desktop with a high resolution (800x600 or higher), try dragging it to the desktop. Hey, you now have a floating toolbar on your desktop. Resize this properly and place it where you do not have icons interfering. The catch about this trick is that when you click on the "Show Desktop" Button on the taskbar, the toolbar will disappear as well. Click on the Button again to restore it.

Keeping It Clean

Dump your start menu shortcuts into manageable folders. Put all you games into one folder. Place all your stand -alone system utilities under System Tools. Group all your MS Office applications under another folder. You get what we mean. It will clear up the start menu and you will not have to scroll to the bottom just to launch a program. If you have many first-level items on your start menu, use small icons instead by right clicking the

Taskbar|Properties. Place only your really needs on the first-level

Control Panel	: Control Panel.{21EC2020-3AEA-1069-A2DD-08002B30309D}
Dial Up Network	: Dial Up Net.{992CFFA0-F557-101A-88EC-00DD010CCC48}
Printers	: Printers.{2227A280-3AEA-1069-A2DE-08002B30309D}
Recycle Bin	: Recycle Bin.{645FF040-5081-101B-9F08-00AA002F954E}
Subscriptions	: Subscriptions.{F5175861-2688-11d0-9C5E-00AA00A45957}
Font	: Fonts.{BD84B380-8CA2-1069-AB1D-08000948F534}
History	: History.{FF393560-C2A7-11CF-BFF4-444553540000}

of the start menu.

If you really have dozens of single items, place them neatly on the taskbar. That is what toolbars are for. They are faster than the start menu anyway. However, use it sparingly. Too many items on the toolbar will also crowd the taskbar.

Remember; try to avoid applications nesting in the system tray. The system try is only for applications running in background. If the icon at the system tray is just a quick link to the application, use toolbar Button s instead.

Adding Special Cascading Items

Well, there are several things, which you can actually add to the Start menu. However, they need a special CLSID. To add control panel to your start menu, add a folder named Control Panel.{21EC2020-3AEA-1069-A2DD-08002B30309D} and a cascading control panel will appear in your start menu. These are the list of special items you can add to your start menu:

You may change the names in front of the numbers and the names will appear in the start menu. You can also drag them (IE4 installed) to the section between Programs and Run and place it there for easier access. The good thing about this is you can access all of them without the pain of going through the desktop.

Moving About And **Copying Shortcuts**

You can move items that are already in your Start menu by dragging and dropping in Windows 98. You simply point to an item in your Start menu, click the left mouse Button , and hold it down as you drag. As with adding a Shortcut, when hovering over a submenu item it opens that submenu, and Windows displays a divider to indicate where the item would appear if you dropped it. To copy a menu item rather than move it, hold down the Ctrl key as you release the mouse Button.

Advanced Run Features

After the Address bar comes into the taskbar, you will find that you use the Run menu less and less. However, there are still some cool undocumented tricks with the Run menu.

Drag-&-Drop File Names

If you have one icon and you are not quite sure of the full path or extension, just drag it to the Run menu and the full path will appear.

Faster Access

If you have a Windows 95 compatible Keyboard , pressing the Winkey+R will bring up the Run menu, faster than anything else.

Cool Keys

Now you might not know of some fine things to type on the Run menu.

. opens the desktop in a window
.. opens the Windows folder
/ brings you to your C:\ directory

No Full Path Required

Sure, who likes to type the full path? Accessing files and folders had never been easier. For all files in the C:\Windows or your root directory, just type in the filename for example explorer.exe and Windows will just swallow the whole command. However, if you want to specify whether it is the root directory or the C:\Windows directory, just add a / in front of the file or folder in the root directory

Dr Watson To The Rescue

From Windows 3.1 back to Windows 98 after the mysterious disappearance from Windows 95. Dr Watson has now a more user-friendly interface and can do more diagnosis that you thought.

Dr Watson has now a more user-friendly interface and can do more diagnosis that you thought. Dr Watson will generate a snapshot or a rough "image" of what your current system looks like. Then, it will report whether there are anything unusual about your system. Amazingly, this useful utility is well hidden under your C:\Windows\System directory. To launch Dr Watson:

Select Run and type: drwatson.exe

Dr Watson will also intercept any errors like GPF faults under Windows and crash proof your system. Create a shortcut to Dr Watson and add it to your Start up folder for more system stability.

Chapter 31

Windows NT for Beginners

How to cheat at Minesweeper

This tip also works with Windows 2000 & Windows NT 4.0. Who has ever won to Minesweeper? If you are tired of losing all the time, you can try this nice cheat that will basically reveals mines:

1. Start Minesweeper,

2. Type "xyzzy" without the quotes,

3. Hit Shift and Enter at the same time,

4. Minimize all application windows that hide the desktop. The uppermost pixel in the top left corner of your desktop will turn black when you mouse over a mine, and white when it is safe to click.

Windows NT Easter Eggs

Usually after creating software, the computer programmers will include a credit screen. However, they are usually hidden, like an Easter Egg. These are the list of Easter eggs you can find in common software.

Windows NT 4

3D Text Screen Saver Easter Egg

1. Go to Control Panel/Display/Screen Saver and select "3D Text" as your screen saver.
2. Click on "Settings" and change the text to be displayed to:
· I love NT - displays the word 'good?'
· Volcano - displays different volcano names.
· not evil - displays a list of developers.

Windows NT 3.51 Workstation

3D Text Screen Saver Easter Egg

1. Go to Control Panel/Display/Screen Saver and select "3D Text" as your screen saver.
2. Click on "Settings" and change the text to be displayed:
· I love NT - displays a list of developers.
· BEER - displays a list of beers.
· Rock - displays a list of rock bands.

3D Pipes Screen Saver Easter Egg
1. Choose 3D Pipes as your screen saver.
2. Click "Settings" and choose Mixed Joint Styles.
3. When the screen saver runs, teapots will appear randomly as joints in the pipes.

Windows NT 3.5x Server

User Manager Easter Egg
1. Run User Manager for Domains.
2. Make sure CAPS LOCK is on.
3. Type NTLAN. Some fake users should appear.
4. Try typing it again.
5. Exit User Manager to delete them.

Think Before You Convert

NTFS is a robust and secure disk-operating environment. However, no operating system other than NT can read an NTFS partition, and once you have converted a FAT, or FAT32 partition to NTFS, there is no going back. So think hard before you convert. If your system has only one hard disk partition and you want to dual-boot, stay with the old FAT system.

NT Will not Boot For Me

If Windows NT will not boot properly and you know what file or driver may be causing the problem, you can boot your computer using a DOS system disk. Your computer will boot to a DOS prompt, and as long as you are not using NTFS, you can remove the offending file manually.

Creating an NT Repair Disk

You can create an emergency repair disk by going to the System32 folder in your NT folder from Explorer: double-click the rdisk icon or type rdisk.exe at the Run prompt. This will start the Repair Disk utility, which allows you to either create a new repair disk or update an old one.

Weird NT Behavior

If you have just made a change to your Windows NT environment and it starts behaving erratically, restart your computer. When you get the message 'Press the Space Bar to use Last Known Good Installation', do so. Your PC will boot to the configuration made before your last change to the NT environment.

Add New Options To The Right Click In Windows NT 4.0

When you right click on a file in Explorer, the choices for that extension are presented. To add a new choice, select view/options/File Types. Scroll to the file type you wish to use, select it, and click the Edit Button. Click the New Button. Type the "Action" (Edit, Smile, Print, view,) and the full path to the application (and any commandline switches/parameters) required to perform the "Action". If you want to change an "Action", click "Edit" instead of "New". I suggest you edit the "Actions" of "Text Document", "Write Document" and any type that uses DDE such as "Microsoft Word Document" to see the possibilities.

Lock Those Files

By default, Windows NT gives full access to anyone who can log on to your computer. However, if you are using NTFS, you can prevent other people from accessing files and folders that you created yourself--and if you are logged on as the administrator, you do not even need to be their creator. Right-click the file or folder that you want to set access privileges for and choose Properties. Click the Security tab and then click Permissions. To remove a user, select a name and click Remove. To add groups of users (for example, by department), click Add and select from the list provided.

Adding Specific Applications To Your Send-To Folder

When you right click on a file in explorer, you can choose to Open with or Send To. You can add applications to your Send To. Create a Shortcut to your application (right click the NameOfProgram.exe) and copy (or cut) the Shortcut to %windir%\Profiles\YourUserId\SendTo.
Now, when you right click on that file with a non-stand port extension, you can Send To your application.

Registry Editing Tips

Creating a Logon Warning Message

To create a login warning message (such as one reading "For Business Use Only, Unauthorized use is prohibited."), do the following

1. Start RegEdit (regedt32.exe)
2. Move down to HKEY_LOCAL_MACHINE/Software/Microsoft/Windows NT/Current Version/Winlogin
3. Edit the following items:
· LegalNoticeCaption
· LegalNoticeText

Automatically Log On a User when NT Boots

For NT 3.51:
Use REGEDT32.EXE, and search for the key HKEY_LOCAL_MACHINE\SOFTWARE\Microsoft\Windows NT\CurrentVersion\Winlogon. Fill in the keys DefaultDomainName, DefaultUserName, and DefaultPassword with the values of the already-established Windows NT user. You may have to add the DefaultPassword key.
Then choose Add Value from the menu and add a new key, named AutoAdminLogon. Select REG_SZ for the Data Type. Enter "1" (without the quotes) in the String field.
Save the changes and restart - Windows NT should automatically log the system on as that user.

For NT 4.0:
The Method above does not work properly with NT 4.0. The easiest method is to simply download the Microsoft TWEAKUI PowerToy. It has a tab labeled "NETWORK" that allows you to specify what user id and password you want NT 4.0 to automatically use for logging on during the boot process.
NOTE: This can be a BIG security problem - only use it on machines that are physically secured.

Moving a profile from a workgroup to a domain

you have been using a workgroup setup and now are moving to a Domain setup. The users have desktop settings and you would like to keep these when they login as a domain user However, the settings are lost.

Log in with the local userID on the machine, open REGEDIT.EXE, select the \HKey_Current_Uuser key, and choose Registry|Export registry. The user can then use the resulting .reg file after he logs in to his domain account, just dbl clicking on it. That will transfer the settings. Make sure he has full rights to his \HKey_Current_User key of the registry

Disabling CD-ROM "autorun" under NT

To disable CD Autorun:

1. Start RegEdit (regedt32.exe)
2. Go to
HKEY_LOCAL_MACHINE/System/CurrentControlSet/Services/ Cdrom
3. Edit the following item:
· Autorun: set to 0 (zero).

Increase Your Logon Security

By default, Windows NT 4.0 displays the name of the last person who logged on the system. This can pose a security threat, especially if a user's password can be guessed from the account name or the login environment. To turn this "feature" off take the following steps:

1. Launch the Registry editor. (regedt32)
2. Go to Hkey_Local_Machine key.
3. Locate the

Subkey\Software\Microsoft\WindowsNT\CurrentVersion\Winlogo
n.
4. Select the ReportBootOK item.
5. Select Edit/New/String Value from the menu bar.
6. Type DontDisplayLastUserName for the string's name.
7. Double-click the new string to edit its value.
8. Change the value to 1.
9. Click OK.
10. Close the Registry editor.

Does Your CD-Rom Changer Cycle A Lot?

If your CD-ROM Changer cycles excessively, try out this tip below.

1. Set HKEY_LOCAL_MACHINE\SYSTEM\CurrentControlSet \Services\Cdrom\Autorun to zero.
2. Set the "Start Up" of CD Audio in Control Panel / Devices to Manual. Press the Stop Button (This may not be required on your installation).
3. Create a shortcut to Explorer (set to minimized) and place it in your Startup folder. Leave it minimized. It will share the CD information with all other copies of Explorer that you open and with all properly written applications.

Chapter 32

Windows ME for Beginners

Introduction

A few months after the successful release of Windows 2000 in full flare, Microsoft unveils the brand new consumer focused edition of Windows, an evolution of Windows 98, named Windows

Millennium Edition. This new version is, according to Microsoft, the ultimate evolution of the Windows 9x OS family and carries the build number 4.90.3000. Indeed future Windows releases should be based on the NT kernel.

The Millennium edition of Windows is aimed to help PC home users to enter into the next millennium with a big bang as Microsoft has focused its efforts to make Windows Me the user-friendliest, easy-to-use and multimedia-rich operating system of all the time. Windows Me has been developed and tested by Microsoft numerous months to ensure its reliability However, does it have what it takes to make you want to pay out more money for a operating system that may well be too similar to Windows 98 and Windows 98 SE. Read on for our comprehensive review of this new operating system, Microsoft Windows Millennium Edition (Win Me). Here is a list of most of the features that make up Windows Me (Note that these features are written on the MS Press release, not our write up):

Digital Media:

Edit, catalog, and e-mail your home movies

Windows Movie Maker makes it easy to transfer home movies to your computer. You can edit audio and video sequences from analog and digital cameras, VCRs, or the Web, then create home-video shorts that you can e-mail to friends, relatives, and colleagues. You can also store hours of video on your hard drive, instead of on the shelf.

Store, manipulate, and organize pictures on your computer without any additional software; you can import a picture from a digital camera or scanner onto your computer. And before you save anything onto your hard drive, you will be able to preview all your photos and delete the ones you do not want.

Play your favorite music and **listen to the radio online**

With one player, experience the most popular streaming and local audio and video formats. You can organize and catalog your media, then easily transfer your play lists to portable devices. If you tire of your music collection, listen to any of the 3,000 Internet radio stations worldwide. You will also be able to revamp the look of your Windows Media™ Player into everything from a shark's head to a television.

Transfer pictures onto your computer in two easy steps

Without any additional software, you can import a picture from a digital camera onto your computer. And before you save anything onto your hard drive, you will be able to preview all your photos and delete the ones you do not want.

Immerse yourself in dynamic 3-D and **surround-sound**

DirectX® 7 intensifies the sights and sounds of all your games, delivering the ultimate realism in ambient gaming. Microsoft® DirectX makes Windows-based computers an ideal platform for running and displaying each element of any multimedia composition including full-color graphics, video, 3-D animation, and surround sound.

Home Experience

Learn everything about your operating system, fast

Integrated with online support, the Help and Support system in Windows Me is a comprehensive, Web-based resource that provides tutorials, tours, answers, and solutions to common problems and questions. If you get Windows Me preinstalled on your computer, your manufacturer may also include system-specific support in the Help and Support area.

Your critical files are always safe

The System File Protection feature in Windows Me prevents erroneous system file deletion.

Return your computer to its original settings

If you make a mistake with your settings and want to return your computer to a time and day when everything operated perfectly, simply activate System Restore. When you restart your computer, it will operate as it did prior to any problems.

Install the latest hard **ware, worry free**

You will appreciate no-error installation and the start-to-finish guidance of the Windows Me wizard s. When you install Windows Me, it automatically loads all the Universal Serial Bus (USB) and IEEE 1394 software drivers. Then, when you install a new USB or IEEE 1394 device, Windows Me will find the appropriate driver and automatically install it for you. Wizard s guide you through the installations, and Windows Me instantly configures most devices so you do not have to restart your computer or tweak your settings.

Quickly find what you need on every menu

The Smart Menus in Windows Me get to know how you work. They prominently display the programs and applications you use most often, and keep lesser-opened menu items out of site However, readily available. That saves you time you would otherwise have spent searching your menu's contents.

Be assured that your drivers will work with new hard **ware**

For your protection, the Windows Me development team has worked with industry partners to ensure that drivers—the software that makes devices work with your computer—are designed and tested to work with Windows Me. When you hook up a new piece of hard ware, Windows Me runs a driver check to make sure it is digitally signed and capable of working on your computer.

The latest system updates are regularly delivered to your desktop

For your machine to work at peak efficiency with the latest hard ware and software, you will want to update Windows Me from time to time. Windows Me is designed to deliver critical updates directly to your desktop from the Windows Update Web site. You will receive the most recent service packs, system files, device drivers, and new features as often as you like.

Online Experience

Browse the Internet quickly and easily

Internet Explorer 5.5 provides the best support for Web browsing, with powerful search capabilities, faster performance, and easier printing.

Communicate using Web-integrated e-mail, messaging, and news. Outlook® Express lets you send and receive e-mail, access your Hotmail® account, join newsgroups, view your online contacts, and send instant messages—all from one convenient place on your desktop.

Send instant messages

MSN™ Messenger lets you know when your friends are connected to the Internet, so you can exchange instant messages, chat in real time with several friends at once, or hold a video conference using NetMeeting® conferencing software.

Have online video conversations

Using NetMeeting 3.1, you can participate in video conferences, collaborate on files, and share information over the Internet or a local network.

Play games on the Internet

You will find Internet-ready versions of popular, classic games like backgammon, hearts, spades, and checkers. One click gives you instant access to online opponents from around the world.

Home Networking

Create a home network

The process of setting up your home network is simple when you use the step-by-step instructions provided by the Home Networking wizard.

Share a single Internet connection

Internet Connection Sharing (ICS) lets you share a single Internet connection among multiple computers in your home, even if they are running Windows 95 or Windows 98.

Use multiple networking technologies

Windows Me provides support for multiple types of home networking technologies, including Ethernet, wireless, and HomePNA, and lets you view these networks through a single interface.

Share computing resources throughout your home network

Windows Me automatically detects printers, folders, and other resources on your home network, and allows you to easily share these and other resources among the computers on your network.

Incorporate Universal Plug and Play (UPnP) devices

Windows Me is the first operating system to implement UPnP networking stand port s, making it simple to connect all kinds of high-tech appliances, gadgets, wireless devices, and computers to your home network.

Connect to the Internet securely

The new TCP/IP stack in Windows Me provides improved stability and security on the Internet.

How can I bypass the bothering setup floppy creation screen?

Even if it is strongly advised to create a boot floppy under Windows Me due to the removal of the real mode, DOS you can bypass the screen of the setup that will ask you to create such a disk. To do so simply run the setup under DOS or Windows 9x like this: 'setup.exe /ie'. You can also just click cancel when it asks you to insert a floppy during the setup if you like.

Is there a way to bypass the Pentium 150 setup limitation?

Windows Me is build to be run at least on a Pentium 150Mhz processor. That is why when you try to install it on a Pentium 133 you receive an error message saying your computer is not powerful enough. If you think your computer is powerful enough to use Windows Me and if you are a patient guy then launch the Windows Me setup with this commandline: setup.exe /NM

How can I ignore the Scandisk check process of the Win Me setup?

Well the Scandisk checkup of the Windows Me setup is quite bothering, particularly if you run the setup from DOS and it takes a lot of time depending on the size of your HD. Therefore, to disable this check simply run the setup with this line command: 'setup.exe /is'

To add or change a device driver

•   Open System properties in Control Panel.
•   Click the Device Manager tab, click the plus sign next to the type of hard ware, and Click the Driver tab, click Update Driver, and then follow the instructions on the screen.

To reserve disk space for extra memory

•   Open System properties in Control Panel.
•   Click the Performance tab, and then click Virtual Memory.
•   Make sure Let Windows manage my virtual memory settings is selected.

To undo a system restoration

• You can undo your last restoration, or you can choose restoration points prior to the last restoration.
• Click Start, point to Programs, point to Accessories, and point to System Tools, and then click System Restore. Do one of the following:
• To undo your last restoration, click Undo my last restoration. Close any open programs, and then click Next.
• To roll back to another restore point, click Start the System Restore wizard, and then follow the instructions on your screen.

Did you know that in Windows ME you could run programs from the Address bar in the browser?

The next time you are surfing the Web and want to run a program such as Microsoft Word, just type the program name (including its path) in the Address bar, and then press ENTER. For example, you might type C:\Program Files\Microsoft Office\Office\winword.exe.

Roll back the clock with System Restore

Theoretical physicist Stephen Hawking writes that each of us carries a personal measure of time dependent on our speed and position in the universe. When you find that your computer is not working the way it should, you may also find that your personal measure of time has come to a complete stop, and that your productivity has disappeared into a black hole.

With System Restore, Windows Me gives you the power to pull yourself out. This powerful utility will propel you back to a time when your computer was working without incident.

Take a picture

Instead of wading through documentation or waiting for a support technician to devise a fix, System Restore lets you set your computer back to a time when it was working without incident— for example, before you downloaded that Bop the Clown game from the Web site you did not know anything about. System Restore makes a snapshot of your computer's configurations, files, settings, and data. It then tightly compresses this snapshot and stores it on your hard disk, creating a restore point that you can revert to in times of computer crisis.

System Restore creates a restore point every 10 hours that your computer is on, and every 24 hours of real time. If your computer has been off for more than 24 hours, System Restore will create a restore point when you start up. You can also create your own point manually.

To set up a manual restore point:

Click the Start Button.

Point to Programs, point to Accessories, point to System Tools, and then click System Restore.

Choose Create a restore point, and then click Next.

In the Restore point description box, type a name for your restore point, and then click Next.

Click OK.

Travel through time

Once you have restore points configured, it is easy to revert to them. do not worry about losing information in recent documents or e-mail messages, as System Restore does not alter your personal files. You also have the option of reversing any changes that System Restore makes to your computer.

To restore your computer settings from an earlier time:

Click the Start Button.

Point to Programs, point to Accessories, point to System Tools, and then click System Restore.

Choose Restore my computer to an earlier time, and then click Next.

Click a day on the calendar, click the restore point description, and then click Next.

Make sure you have closed all your files and open programs, and then click OK to close the dialog box.

Click Next.

Your system will revert to its previous settings, your time will return to its usual dimensions, and you can go full speed ahead.

Create a Windows Me startup disk

Despite its awesome power, your computer is not impervious to certain perils, whether caused by a computer virus, software downloaded from the Web, or simply general wear. Even a small hard disk problem may cause you to lose days or even months of your hard work.

In the event a problem prevents you from starting Windows Me, you can use a Windows Me startup disk, also called a "boot disk", to start your computer, gain access to your system files, run diagnostic programs, and fix problems. It can be an ounce (or a megabyte) of prevention, should your hard disk fall on hard times.

Give startup problems the boot.
You can use the Windows Me startup disk to start your computer from its floppy drive if it will not start from the hard drive. Using the disk, you can get your computer running again, so you can start fixing what is wrong. The startup disk will also restore minimal display settings, to ensure that you are able to see you're desktop. The disk contains:

 CD-ROM drivers that allow your CD-ROM drive to function if your computer is having problems communicating with it. Small Computer System Interface (SCSI) drivers, which work with your hard drive and some peripherals. System and diagnostic programs, such as Scandisk, that check your hard disk for errors and help diagnose problems after you get your computer started.

How to create a startup disk

Normally, you would create a startup disk when you installed

Windows Me. If your startup disk is old (from an earlier version of Windows), you will need to make a new startup disk for Windows Me. If you never made a startup disk, or if you have lost it, now is a great time to make a new one. It is easy.

To create a boot disk, you will need a blank, 1.2-megabyte (MB) disk. You may also need your Windows Me CD, so be sure to have it handy To create a startup disk:

1. Click Start, point to Settings, click Control Panel, and then click Add/Remove Programs.

2. Click the Startup Disk tab, and then click Create Disk.

3. Label a floppy disk "Windows Me Startup Disk", insert the disk in your floppy drive when prompted, and then click OK. Windows Me will begin to copy files to the floppy disk.

4. When copying is complete, click OK, and then store the disk in a safe place

Customize Windows Media Player

Say it is a gray day, and you would like nothing better than the blues. With Windows Media Player, you can download blues music, find a blues radio station, apply a blue skin to your player, choose a blue light show, and immerse yourself in indigo. Windows Media Player's special effects let you change its look (and mood) to fit the music. Here are some of the ways in which you can customize Windows Media Player.

•   Switch between modes to change the size of the player.

•   Apply a skin to change the way the player looks.

•   Choose a visualization to enhance the beat of your music.

When you first open Windows Media Player, it is in Full Mode. To save space on your desktop, you can shrink the size of the player by switching to compact mode. Just click the arrow icon in the lower right-hand corner, or click Compact Mode in the View menu. If you have chosen visualization, it will remain when you switch to Compact Mode. When you apply a skin, Windows Media Player automatically switches to Compact Mode.

Want to change the way Windows Media Player looks? Click the Skin Chooser Button and go wild. Click the skin titles in the list to see what each looks like. If you find one that suits your fancy, click the Apply Skin Button. The Windows Media Player will morph into its new identity.

Some of the skins feature a display area for playing visualizations—so if you want to see your groovy lights, be sure the skin you choose includes a blank screen. Also, you may find that the player Button s have moved into new places after you apply a skin. do not worry. You can easily return to Full Mode by clicking the arrow Button on the skin or the gray arrow Button in the lower right-hand corner of your screen.

If you do not like the skins, it is easy to find a new one at WindowsMedia.com:

1. In Skin Chooser in Windows Media Player, click the More Skins Button. The WindowsMedia.com Web site will open.

2. Browse through the lists of skins (you will find several pages of them), until you find the one you want.

3. Click the name of the skin you want to apply to download it.

4. When the download is complete, click the View Now Button to open the player with the skin applied, or click the Close Button to return to Windows Media Player in Full Mode. (If you click the Close Button, you can view the new skin by clicking the skin name, and then clicking the Apply Skin Button at the top of the list.)

A moving accompaniment

While you are listening to your favorite tunes, you can enjoy your own customized light show. Windows Media Player offers an array of dreamy visualizations to suit your music and your mood. To visualize your music:

1. Select a song from the Media Library.
2. Click the Now Playing Button.
3. Click the arrow Button s to change the visualization.
4. For a new collection of visualizations, click the View menu, highlight Visualizations, and then click the visualization you want from the list that appears.

Whether you want to play your R & B CDs or listen to news radio from France, Windows Media Player lets you listen to (and see) the music you want, exactly the way you want it.

Starting with Windows Movie Maker

Windows Movie Maker is the exciting new feature in Windows Me that lets you record, store, organize, edit, and share your home movies.

You could be taking meetings in Hollywood or hobnobbing at the Sundance Film Festival before you know it. For novice and even intermediate home computer users, however, your first adventure with Windows Movie Maker could very well be a journey into the heart of your computer.

The wide range of hard ware configurations—for both video equipment and home computers—has created an equally wide range of hard ware compatibility scenarios. The way your system works with Windows Movie Maker depends on the equipment that you own.

There are essentially only two situations, one based on using your computer and Windows Me with analog video equipment, and the other based on doing the same with digital video equipment.

Analog video equipment

For analog video cameras and VCRs, the all-important interfacing device you are likely to need is an analog USB audio/video capture device, sometimes known as a "dongle." This is a small, simple device that connects to a USB port on your computer and allows you to attach audio and video cables from your video camera or VCR.

Some analog video cameras and VCRs are supported by a video capture card, which you may need to install if your computer does not already have one. Video capture cards can improve the quality of your video as it is converted from analog to digital format, However, finding the right one and installing it may require some help from an experienced computer user.

And some video capture card s provide the ability to attach audio and video cables from your video camera or VCR directly to your computer, which means you will not need a dongle. Check your video capture card documentation to find out if this is possible for you.

Digital video cameras

Digital video cameras require an IEEE 1394 connection, which is not currently a stand port part of most home computer systems. Consult your system profile to see if your computer has IEEE 1394 capability. If it doesn't, you will need to install an interface card (sometimes referred to as a "firewire" card). To find the right card, you can start by contacting the manufacturer of your computer for information about which cards work with your system. You will also need to contact the manufacturer of your video camera for recommendations on the best IEEE 1394 cards to work with your camera.

Note It is important to find an interface card that works with both your computer and your video camera.

After you have found the appropriate card, you will need to install it, which requires you to remove the casing from your computer and snap the card into place. It is a fairly simple process; however, it is probably best to get the help of an experienced computer user.

Finally, whether your video equipment is analog or digital, you will need a driver to keep all the different parts working together correctly. A driver is a small piece of software that, in this case, allows your video equipment to work with the capture card in your computer. Check the Web site of the manufacturer of your video equipment to make sure the appropriate driver is available. If it is not, you may need to call or write the manufacturer to find out when it will be available. Many IEEE 1394 interface card drivers are already installed with Windows Me.

Windows Movie Maker: Get your film in the can

Whether you are stitching together pieces of your home movies for friends and relatives to enjoy, or have embarked on a budding career as a filmmaker, the first thing you need to do is get your footage out of the camera or off a videocassette and onto your hard disk.

Cut! Print it!
With Windows Movie Maker, it is easy to transfer your video footage to your hard disk so you can begin working with it.

After your video devices have been configured and are ready to go, open Windows Movie Maker and click Record on the toolbar. The resulting Record dialog box offers you a variety of choices, including:

- Which device you want to record from, if more than one is connected.
- Record audio only, video only, or both.
- A recording time limit.
- A general quality level.
- Other recording qualities, such as brightness, contrast, saturation, and more.

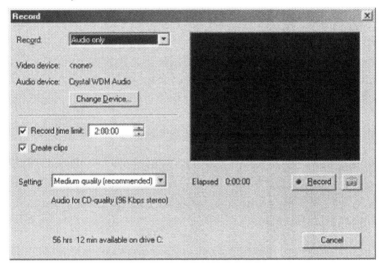

The building blocks of your movie

When recording an hour or more of video from a single source, navigating the footage to find the clips you need can be time-consuming. The shot detection feature in Windows Movie Maker automatically creates separate clips every time an entirely different frame is detected (meaning each time the camera moves from one subject to another). Before you begin recording, select Create clips to enable shot detection.

Keep in mind that clips are the basic building blocks of your movie. The combination of clips, when added and arranged on the storyboard or timeline, will compose your movie.

When you have your settings the way you want them, click Record. The word "Recording" will blink to indicate that you are recording, and the time elapsed for your current recording shows next to it. After recording has begun, the Record Button becomes a Stop Button . Click Stop when you want to stop recording.

Dress up your production

You do not have to stop with just the original video that you have shot. Windows Movie Maker lets you include in your movie existing photos, audio clips, or other video files that you have stored on your computer. You can import many different file types, including:

• Video files with an .asf, .avi, or .wmv file extension.

• Movie files with an .mpeg, .mpg, .m1v, .mp2, .mpa, or .mpe file extension.

• Audio files with a .wav, .snd, .au, .aif, .aifc, .aiff, .wma, or .mp3 file extension.

• Windows Media-based files with an .asf, .wm, .wma, or .wmv file extension.

• Still images with a .bmp, .jpg, .jpeg, .jpe, .jfif, .gif, or .dib file extension.

• PowerPoint files and individual slides with a .ppt extension.

To add one of the above file types to your movie:

1. On the File menu, click Import.

2. Locate the file you want to add. When you import a file, a clip that refers to the file appears in the main window.

Once you have transferred the elements that you want to include in your movie, you can begin organizing and working with them on the storyboard —that is when the real fun starts.

Taskbar basics

The taskbar typically sits at the bottom of your screen, visible at all times. It includes the Start Button and, by default, the Quick Launch bar.

Start at the beginning

Click the Start Button to see the Start menu, which gives you access to your programs, system tools, Windows Help, and more. With the Find tool you can search for files on your computer. Favorites gives you instant access to all your favorite documents and Web pages. You can rearrange programs on the Start menu any way you like.

Quick Launch for fast access

The Quick Launch bar sits just to the right of the Start Button. From the Quick Launch bar, you can open frequently used programs. Each icon on it represents a program or tool on your computer. There is even an icon for the desktop, which you can click to minimize all your open programs. You can add the programs you use most often: Click Start, and then point to Programs. Click and drag the program you want to add to the Quick Launch area in the taskbar.

Keep track of your work

The taskbar also keeps track of all your open programs and documents. Each time you open a program, a corresponding Button appears on the taskbar. To switch between programs, just click the Button for the program you want. To minimize an open window, click its Button on the taskbar. Click once to minimize; click again to restore the window to your screen. You can also use the taskbar Button s to close several programs at once.

Set your clock

The clock is on the far right of the taskbar. Double-click the clock to open the Date/Time Properties dialog box, where you can change the date, time, and time zone.

Move and size the taskbar

You can drag the taskbar to the top or either side of your desktop, or change its size by dragging its edges

Chapter 33

Windows 2000 for Beginners

How to view and print a fax
1. Click Start, click Programs, click Accessories, click Communications, click Fax, and then click My Faxes.
2. In the My Faxes folder, double-click either Received Faxes or Sent Faxes.
3. Double-click the fax you want to view or print. The fax is displayed in the Imaging Preview viewer. If you want to print the fax, on the File menu, click Print

Adding A Color Profile To A Printer

Open Printers.
Right-click the printer that you want to associate with a color profile, click Properties, and then click the Color Management tab. Click Add to open the Add Profile Association dialog box.

Locate the new color profile you want to associate with the printer.

Preview An Image Or Picture

Open Windows Explorer.
Double-click the folder that contains your pictures.
If your pictures are stored in the My Pictures folder, click the name of the picture you want to preview. The picture appears in the Image Preview window to the left of your file list.
If your pictures are not stored in the My Pictures folder, click the View menu, click Customize This Folder, and then follow the rest of this procedure.

In the Customize This Folder wizard, click Next, select Choose or edit an HTML template, and then click Next again.
In Choose a template, click Image Preview, and then follow the instructions on your screen to complete the wizard and turn on Image Preview.
Click the name of the image you want to preview
Using Personalized Menus

Personalized Menus keeps the Programs menu clean by hiding items you have not used recently, while keeping all of your programs easily accessible.

When Personalized Menus is turned on, Windows 2000 keeps track of which programs you use each time you use your computer, and hides the programs you have not used in a long time.

You can still gain access to hidden programs by clicking Start, pointing to Programs, and then clicking the down arrow at the bottom of the menu.

To turn on Personalized Menus, click Start, point to Settings, click Taskbar & Start Menu, and then select Use Personalized Menus on the General tab.

How to turn on FilterKeys

Open Accessibility Options in Control Panel.
On the Keyboard tab, under FilterKeys, select the Use FilterKeys
check box.

To open Accessibility Options, click Start, point to Settings, click
Control Panel, and then double-click Accessibility Options.
To change the settings for Filter Keys, on the Keyboard tab,
under FilterKeys, click Settings.

If the Use shortcut check box in the Settings for FilterKeys dialog
box is selected, you can turn FilterKeys on and off by holding
down the right SHIFT key for 8 to 16 seconds (depending on the
other settings you have selected in the Accessibility Options dialog
box).
How to turn on Show Sounds

Open Accessibility Options in Control Panel.
On the Sound tab, under Show Sounds, select the Use Show
Sounds check box.

How to add a program to the Quick Launch bar

In My Computer or Windows Explorer, click the icon for the
program you want to add, and drag it to the Quick Launch portion
of the taskbar.

The icon for that program appears next to the other Quick Launch
icons on the taskbar.
Adding A Color Profile To A Monitor

Open Display in Control Panel.
On the Settings tab, click Advanced.

On the Color Management tab, click Add to open the Add Profile Association dialog box.
Locate the new color profile you want to associate with the monitor.

Click the new profile, and then click Add.
How To Find System Data

Open System Information.
On the Action menu, click Find.
In Find What, type the word or words corresponding to the system information for which you are searching.
Select a search option as needed.

To search only through the portion of the console tree, click Restrict Search to Selected Category. This option starts the search at the top of the currently selected node (and searches all of its subcategories). Clearing this check box starts the search at the root node.

To search only the console tree node and sub node names for a match, ignoring any matches in the results pane, click Search Categories Only. Clearing this check box searches both the console tree and the results pane.

To search all categories and results information clear both check boxes.

How to turn on StickyKeys

Open Accessibility Options in Control Panel.
On the Keyboard   tab, under StickyKeys, select the Use StickyKeys check box.
 Notes

To open Accessibility Options, click Start, point to Settings, click Control Panel, and then double-click Accessibility Options.
To change settings for StickyKeys, on the Keyboard tab, under StickyKeys, click Settings.
How to turn on SoundSentry

Open Accessibility Options in Control Panel.
On the Sound tab, under SoundSentry, select the Use SoundSentry check box.

How to compose a document using multiple languages

Create or open a document

In the status area on the taskbar, click the input locale indicator located near the system time, and then click the language you want to use to compose.

Compose your document.
To change languages, click the input locale indicator on the taskbar, and then click another language from the list.
How to compose a document using multiple languages

General

How do I check to see how long Windows 2000 has been up?

Use the commandline utility called UPTIME. You can also use it to check remote machines.

UPTIME, Version 1.00
(C) Copyright 1999, Microsoft Corporation

Uptime [server] [/s] [/a] [/d:mm/dd/yyyy | /p:n] [/heartbeat] [/? | /help]
    server   Name or IP address of remote server to process.

/s	Display key system events and statistics.
/a	Display application failure events (assumes /s).
/d:	Only calculate for events after mm/dd/yyyy.
/p:	Only calculate for events in the previous n days.
/heartbeat	Turn on/off the system's heartbeat
/?	Basic usage.
/help	Additional usage information.

How to suppress personal cover pages

Open Fax Service Management.
Right-click Fax Service on Local Computer, and then click Properties.

On the General tab, select the do no tallow personal cover pages check box.

How to set ownership on drives

Open Computer Management (Local).
In the console tree, click Logical Drives.
Computer Management (Local)

Storage

Logical Drives

mso-list:l11 level1 lfo1;tab-stops:list 36.0pt">Right-click the drive for which you want to set ownership, click Properties, and then click the Security tab.
mso-list:l11 level1 lfo1;tab-stops:list 36.0pt">Click Advanced, and then click the Owners tab.
mso-list:l11 level1 lfo1;tab-stops:list 36.0pt">Click the new owner, and then click OK.

You must be logged on as an administrator or a member of the Administrators group in order to complete this procedure. If your computer is connected to a network, network policy settings may also prevent you from completing this procedure.
To open Computer Management, click Start, point to Settings, and then click Control Panel. Double-click Administrative Tools, and then double-click Computer Management.
You can only change ownership on drives formatted to use NTFS. You can change ownership settings on a remote computer or a local computer. To access a remote computer, right-click Computer Management (Local), click Connect to another computer, and then select the computer you want to connect to.
Logical Drives only changes ownership of the drive, not the folders and files on the drive.
How To Set The Magnification Level

Open Magnifier.

In the Magnifier dialog box, select an up or down arrow in Magnification level to increase or decrease magnification by number. The default magnification level is 2
How to pause or resume an outgoing queue

Open Computer Management.

In the console tree, right-click Outgoing Queues.
Computer Management
Services and Applications
Message Queuing
Outgoing Queues
Click Pause.
Or, to resume the operation of the queue, click Resume.

How to enable RIP Listening

Click Start, point to Settings, click Control Panel, and then double-click Add/Remove Programs.
Click Add/Remove Windows Components.
In Components, select Networking Services (However, do not select its check box), and then click Details.
Select the RIP Listener check box, and then click OK.
Click Next, and then follow the instructions in the wizard.

How to set special access configuration permissions for DCOM programs

Open Distributed COM Configuration Properties.
Click the Default Security tab, under Default Configuration Permissions click Edit Default.
In Registry Key Permissions in Type of Access, click Special Access.

In the Special Access dialog box, click the type of control you want to assign to the selected user or group:
To assign Full Control, click Full Control (All).
To customize special access, click Other, and then click the types of access that you want to assign.

To enable the user to read a value entry from the registry key, click Query Value.

To enable the user to set value entries in the registry key, click Set Value.
To enable the user to create subkeys on the registry key, click Create Subkey.

To enable the user to identify the subkeys of the registry key, click Enumerate Subkeys.

To enable the user to audit notification events from the key, click Notify.

To enable the user to create a symbolic link in the key, click Create Link.

To enable the user to delete the key, click Delete.
To enable the user to gain access to the key for the purpose of writing a discretionary ACL to the key, click Write DAC.
To enable the user to gain access to the key for the purpose of taking ownership of it, click Write Owner.

To enable the user to gain access to the security information on the key, click Read Control.

How to add a submenu to the Start menu for a group of users

Make sure you are logged on as an administrator.
Right-click Start, and then click Open All Users.
Double-click the folder in which you want to add a submenu, usually the Programs folder.

On the File menu, point to New, and then click Folder.
Type a name for your new submenu, and then click an empty space on the desktop

How to add a submenu to the Start menu for a group of users

Make sure you are logged on as an administrator.
Right-click Start, and then click Open All Users.
Double-click the folder in which you want to add a submenu, usually the Programs folder.

On the File menu, point to New, and then click Folder.
Type a name for your new submenu, and then click an empty space on the desktop

Using wildcard   characters

Asterisk (*)

You can use the asterisk as a substitute for zero or more characters. If you are looking for a file that you know starts with gloss However, you cannot remember the rest of the file name, type the following:

gloss*

The Find dialog box will locate all files of any file type that begin with gloss including Glossary.txt, Glossary.doc, and Glossy.doc. To narrow the search to a specific type of file, type:

gloss*.doc

In this case, the Find dialog box will find all files that begin with gloss However, have the file extension .doc, such as Glossary.doc and Glossy.doc.

Question Mark (?)

You can use the question mark as a substitute for a single character in a name. For example, if you typed gloss?.doc, the Find dialog box would locate the file Glossy.doc or Gloss1.doc However, not Glossary.doc.

How to change the size of the virtual memory paging file

Open System in Control Panel.
On the Advanced tab, click Performance Options, and under Virtual memory, click Change.

In the Drive list, click the drive that contains the paging file you want to change.

Under Paging file size for selected drive, type a new paging file size in megabytes in the Initial size (MB) or Maximum size (MB) box, and then click Set.

If you decrease the size of either the minimum or maximum page file settings, you must restart your computer to see the effects of those changes. Increases typically do not require a restart.
Using The Private Character Editor

You can use Private Character Editor to create unique letters and logos for your font library.

Open Private Character Editor.

Notes

To open Private Character Editor, click Start, click Run, and then type eudcedit.
For information about using Private Character Editor, click the Help menu in Private Character Editor.
How to change the mount order in the work queue

Open Removable Storage.

In the console tree, click Work Queue.
In the details pane, right-click the applicable mounts operation, and then click Re-order Mounts.

In the Change Mount Order dialog box, do one of the following:
To make the selected mount operation the next to be completed, click Move to the front of the queue.

To make the selected mount operation the last to be completed, click Move to the end of the queue.

To move the selected mount operation to a specific position in the work queue, click Make it number, and then click the up or down arrow to move the item ahead or behind in the queue.

How to repair a basic RAID-5 volume (stripe set with parity)

Open Disk Management.

Right-click the RAID-5 volume you want to repair, and then click Repair Volume.

The RAID-5 volume's status should change to Regenerating, then Healthy. If the volume does not return to the Healthy status, right-click the volume and then click Regenerate Parity.

How to convert a volume to NTFS from the commandprompt

Open a commandprompt window.
In the command prompt window, type
convert drive_letter: /fs:ntfs
How to add a program from a network

Open Add/Remove Programs in Control Panel.
Click Add New Programs.

If your computer is connected to a network, the programs you are authorized to add are displayed at the bottom of the screen. If your network administrator has organized programs into categories, you may need to select a different option in Category to see the program you want to add.

Select the program you want to add, and then click Add.
Follow the instructions on your screen.
Adding Themes to Windows 2000

Although there is no tool in Control Panel for configuring desktop themes in Windows 2000, you can use and configure desktop themes by using the Desktop Themes tool.

Click Start, and then click Run,
In the Open box, type themes, and then click OK,
Configure the theme you want, and then click OK.

Registry

Editing The Registry/Rules To Follow

Fiddling about in the Windows 2000 registry can be dangerous to your PC's health to say the least. For a start, you must remember that once you edit a registry key there is no turning back as neither registry editor in Windows 2000 has an undo feature.

Now then, what next? Well Windows 2000 comes with two registry editors for you to try to get to grips with, one is the good old Regedt32.exe, and the other is regedit32.exe an older version of regedit. We will cover what these two do in a later tip However, for now, here are a run down of rules we follow before making a registry edit, we recommend that you do the same.

Back up the registry before performing an edit as there is always the risk of a mistake.

Remember the keys you change just incase you would like to change them back to the original settings.

If you are worried about a setting, you are thinking of changing, the best thing to do is not to change it unless it is vital to do so. How to Enable Auto-Complete Feature In The CommandPrompt

This neat tip, Jamel provided us, avoids headaches when using the commandprompt console. It'll turn on the auto-complete feature so when you type 'cd d' and hit the tab key, the console will display the list of folders that begin with the 'd' letter, and you will be able to choose the one you are looking for, right from the console instead of typing its path.

Log on as Administrator,
Click Start, and then click Run,
Type Regedit and OK,
Double click HKEY_LOCAL_MACHINE,
Double click SOFTWARE,
Double click Microsoft,
Double click CommandProcessor,
In the right pane of Regedit, double click the 'CompletionChar' DWORD value,
Type 9 click OK,
Close Regedit,
Click start/programs/accessories/commandprompt,
Type 'cd d' and hit the Tab key: the first folder that matches the 'd' letter is displayed (you can switch from folders pushing several times the Tab key).
How to Enable Application Compatibility-Mode Technology in Windows 2000 Service Pack 2

Compatibility mode provides an environment for running programs that more closely reflect the behavior of either Microsoft Windows 95 or Microsoft Windows NT 4.0. These modes resolve several of the most common issues that prohibit older programs from working correctly with Windows 2000. Programs that experience issues after migration may benefit from being started in one of these compatibility environments.

Log on as Administrator,
Click Start, and then click Run,
In the Open box, type the following command, and then click OK, where %SystemRoot% is the drive and folder in which Windows 2000 is installed:

regsvr32 %systemroot%\apppatch\slayerui.dll

Administrators can use a program shortcut to set the compatibility mode for a target program. This requires that the Compatibility-mode properties be correctly installed and registered on the computer by using the previous steps. To enable Compatibility mode by using a program shortcut:

Log on as Administrator,
Right-click the shortcut, and then click Properties,
Click the Compatibility tab. This tab appears only if the Compatibility-mode interface has been properly enabled on the computer,

Click to select the Run in Compatibility Mode check box to enable Compatibility-mode support for the program,
Click either Windows 95 or Windows NT 4.0 compatibility mode in the drop-down box,

Click OK to save the changes,
Double-click the shortcut to run the program.

Security, Backup & Recovery

Validate a security configuration file

secedit /validate

This command validates the syntax of a security template you want to import into a database for analysis or application to a system.

Syntax

secedit /validate filename

Parameters

filename

The file name of the security template you have created with Security Templates.

Choosing recovery actions if Windows 2000 stops unexpectedly

Using the Recovery feature in System in Control Panel, you can configure Windows 2000 to do the following when a severe error (called a Stop error or Fatal system error) occurs:

Write an event to the system log.

Alert administrators.
Dump system memory to a file that advanced users can use for debugging.
Automatically restart the computer.
How to change the password for a user

Open Computer Management.

In the console tree, in Local Users and Groups, click Users.
Click the user account change.
Click Action, and then click Set Password.
How to restrict access to author mode in MMC for a domain

Open Active Directory Users and **Computers.**
In the console tree, right-click the organizational unit for which you want to configure policy, and then click Properties.
On the Group Policy tab, click Edit.
The Group Policy console appears.

In the console tree, click Microsoft Management Console.
PolicyName Policy
User Configuration

Administrative Templates

Windows Components

Microsoft Management Console

In the details pane, double-click Restrict the user from entering author mode.

On the Policy tab, do one of the following:

To allow the user to use author mode in MMC, click Not Configured or Disabled.

To restrict the user from using author mode in MMC, click Enabled.

How to restrict access to author mode in MMC for a domain

Open Active Directory Users and Computers.

In the console tree, right-click the organizational unit for which you want to configure policy, and then click Properties.

On the Group Policy tab, click Edit.

The Group Policy console appears.

In the console tree, click Microsoft Management Console.

PolicyName Policy

User Configuration

Administrative Templates

Windows Components

Microsoft Management Console

In the details pane, double-click Restrict the user from entering author mode.

On the Policy tab, do one of the following:

To allow the user to use author mode in MMC, click Not Configured or Disabled.

To restrict the user from using author mode in MMC, click Enabled.

How To Back Up Default Recovery Keys To A Floppy Disk

Click Start, click Run, type mmc /a, and then click OK.

On the Console menu, click Add/Remove Snap-in, and then click Add.

Under Snap-in, click Certificates, and then click Add.

Click My user account, and then click Finish.

Click Close, and then click OK.

Double-click Certificates - User (Administrator), double-click Personal, and then double-click Certificates.

Click the certificate that displays the words File Recovery in the Intended Purposes column.

Right-click the certificate, point to All Tasks, and then click Export.

Follow the instructions in the Certificate Manager Export wizard to export the certificate and associated private key to a .pfx file format. When the wizard   asks for a file name, you can click the Browse Button to point to a location on a floppy disk where you want to save the file. Be sure to store the floppy disk in a secure location.

How to change your password on a NetWare bindery server

Open CommandPrompt.

Change to the drive for the NetWare server, and then type cd \public.

Type setpass, followed by the name of the NetWare server for which you want to change your password.

When prompted for each, type your old password, a new password, and the new password again.

A message confirms that you have successfully changed your password.

If prompted, type y and press ENTER to change your password on other NetWare servers that also use your old password.

Or, to leave your old password unchanged on the other NetWare servers, type n and press ENTER.

To require or disable a logon password in a workgroup setting

Open Users and Passwords in Control Panel.

On the Users tab, do one of the following:

Click the Users must enter a user name and password to use this computer check box to require users to provide this information when they log on.

Clear the Users must enter a user name and password to use this computer check box to allow a user to automatically log on. You will be prompted to provide the name and password of the user who will be automatically logged on each time the computer starts.

How to test IPSec policy integrity

In IP Security Policy Management, click the IP Security Policies on folder.

Click Action, point to All Tasks, and then click Check Policy Integrity.

How to change the password for a user

1. Open Computer Management.
2. In the console tree, in Local Users and Groups, click Users.
3. Click the user account change.

Click Action, and then click Set Password.

Choosing recovery actions if Windows 2000 stops unexpectedly

Using the Recovery feature in System in Control Panel, you can configure Windows 2000 to do the following when a severe error (called a Stop error or Fatal system error) occurs:

- Write an event to the system log.
- Alert administrators.

- Dump system memory to a file that advanced users can use for debugging.

Automatically restart the computer.

Adding Themes to Windows 2000

Although there is no tool in Control Panel for configuring desktop themes in Windows 2000, you can use and configure desktop themes by using the Desktop Themes tool.

1. Click Start, and then click Run,
2. In the Open box, type themes, and then click OK,
3. Configure the theme you want, and then click OK.

How to add a submenu to the Start menu for a group of users

1. Make sure you are logged on as an administrator.
2. Right-click Start, and then click Open All Users.
3. Double-click the folder in which you want to add a submenu, usually the Programs folder.
4. On the File menu, point to New, and then click Folder.

Type a name for your new submenu, and then click an empty space on the desktop

How to add a program from a network

1. Open Add/Remove Programs in Control Panel.
2. Click Add New Programs.

If your computer is connected to a network, the programs you are authorized to add are displayed at the bottom of the screen. If your network administrator has organized programs into categories, you may need to select a different option in Category to see the program you want to add.

3. Select the program you want to add, and then click Add.

Follow the instructions on your screen.

How to pause or resume an outgoing queue

1. Open Computer Management.
2. In the console tree, right-click Outgoing Queues.
   - ○ Computer Management
   - ○ Services and Applications
   - ○ Message Queuing
   - ○ Outgoing Queues
3. Click Pause.

Or, to resume the operation of the queue, click Resume.

How to change the size of the virtual memory paging file

1. Open System in Control Panel.
2. On the Advanced tab, click Performance Options, and under Virtual memory, click Change.
3. In the Drive list, click the drive that contains the paging file you want to change.
4. Under Paging file size for selected drive, type a new paging file size in megabytes in the Initial size (MB) or Maximum size (MB) box, and then click Set.

If you decrease the size of either the minimum or maximum page file settings, you must restart your computer to see defects of those changes. Increases typically do not require a restart.

How to cheat at Minesweeper

Who has ever won to Minesweeper? If you are tired of losing all the time you can try this nice cheat that will basically reveals mines:

1. Start Minesweeper,

2. Type "xyzzy" without the quotes,

3. Hit Shift and Enter at the same time,

4. Minimize all application windows that hide the desktop. The uppermost pixel in the top left corner of your desktop will turn black when you mouse over a mine and white when it is safe to click

Chapter 34

Improve performance of your Windows 2000/XP

You can improve performance of your Windows 2000/XP and reclaim memory by simply disabling the services that is also known as "System Services" you do need to know which Windows 2000 or XP automatically provide by default.

What Are System Services in the 1st place?
System services are actually small helper programs that provide support for other larger programs in Windows 2000.

Many of the services are set up to run automatically each time you start Windows 2000. However, if you are not using the larger programs that these services are designed to support, these services are simply wasting RAM that could be put to better use by your applications. While the word "Disable" is used here to describe the idea that you will remove these services from memory, what you will really be doing is changing the startup setting from Automatic to Manual. When you do, the services will not automatically start each time you launch Windows 2000 Professional. However, Windows 2000 will be able to manually start the services if they are needed. That way you will not be unnecessarily wasting RAM, However, you will notable crippling your system either. Note: If you are running Windows 2000 Professional on a corporate network, you may not be able to adjust system services. Regardless of whether you can or not, you should check with your system administrator before attempting the make these changes.

Changing the startup type of a service from Automatic to Manual is a relatively simple operation. To begin, open the Control Panel, open the Administrative Tools folder, and then double click the Services tool. When you see the Services window, set the View to Detail if it is not already. Then click the Startup Type column header to sort the services by Startup Type. When you do, all the Services that start automatically will appear at the top of the list.

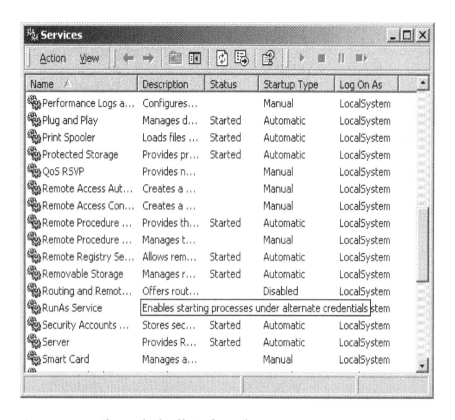

As you scan through the list of services on your system whose Startup Type setting is set to Automatic, look for the services in listed in the Table below. These are some of the services are good candidates to be set to a Manual Startup Type.

Examples of services that can be safely changed to Manual

- **DHCP Client** -- You are not connecting to a specific DHCP server on your local network.
- **Distributed Link Tracking Client** -- You are not connected to a Windows 2000 domain.

- **DNS Client** -- You are not connecting to a specific DNS server on your local network.
- **FTP Publishing Service** -- You do not need your system to act as an FTP server.
- **IIS Admin Service** -- You do not need your system to act as an WWW server.
- **IPSEC Policy Agent** -- You are not connected to a Windows 2000 domain.
- **Messenger** -- You are not connected to a Windows 2000 domain.
- **Remote Registry Service** -- You do not remotely access the Registry of other systems on your local network.
- **RIP Service** -- You do not need your system to act as a router.
- **Run As Service** -- You do not use any applications that run as an alias.
- **World Wide Web Publishing** Service -- You do not need your system to act as a WWW server.

If you find a match and think that your system does not need that particular service, right-click on the service and choose the Properties command from the shortcut menu. When you see, the Properties dialog box for that service, click the Startup Type drop down list, and select Manual. Then click OK. As you change the Startup Type for any service, take note of the service's name. That way you will have a record of which services you changed and can change them back if you need to, as I'll explain in a moment.

Using the Windows Task Manager
Trick: To determine the amount of RAM you will regain by disabling unnecessary system services, use the Windows Task Manager. Here is how: Before you disable any system services, reboot your system and do not launch any applications. If you have applications that automatically load when you start Windows, hold

down the [Shift] key to bypass the Startup folder. Then, right click on the task bar and select Task Manager from the shortcut menu. When you see the Windows Task Manager dialog box, select the Performance tab. Now take note of the Available value in the Physical Memory panel. After you disable those system services, you deem unnecessary, reboot your system in the same manner, and compare the Available value in the Physical Memory panel to the one that you noted earlier.

Final thoughts
Keep in mind that you may not find all the services listed in the Table set to Automatic on your system. In fact, you might not even see some of the services listed present on your system. If that is the case, do not worry about it. Each Windows 2000/XP installation is unique depending on the system and installed software, and different sets of services may be installed and set to start automatically. On the other hand , you may find services other than those listed in Table set to Automatic that you may think are unnecessary. If so, you can find out what each service does by hovering your mouse pointer over the service's description. When you do, a tool tip window will pop up and display the entire description of the service. You can then better determine if the service is unnecessary. Remember, by changing the Startup Type to Manual, Windows 2000 can still start the service if it is needed. If you decide to experiment with changing the Startup Types of certain services, you can monitor the services over time by launching the Services utility and checking the list of running services. If you consistently find one of the services you set to Manual running, you may decide to change the Startup Type back to Automatic.

Chapter 35

Windows XP for Beginners

Windows XP Professional vs. Windows XP Home Edition

Windows XP Professional gives you all the benefits of Windows XP Home Edition, plus additional remote access, security, performance, manageability and multi-lingual features that make it the operating system of choice for businesses of all sizes and people who demand the most out of their computing experience.

Note: "This was taken for Microsoft web page http://www.microsoft.com/windowsxp/home/evaluation/whyupgrade/featurecomp.asp"

Key: ● = Feature included ○ = Feature not included

Features	Windows XP Home Editi	Windows Professio
All the features of Windows XP Home Edition		
▪ New user interface - makes it easy to find what you when you need it. ▪ A reliable foundation you can count on – keeps your computer up and running when you need it most. ▪ Windows Media Player for Windows XP - single pl finding, playing, organizing, & storing digital media. ▪ Network Setup Wizard - easily connect & share the computers and devices in your home. ▪ Windows Messenger – the ultimate communications collaboration tool with instant messaging, voice and video conf and application sharing. ▪ Help & Support Center - easy to recover from probl get help and support when you need it.	●	●

Feature		
Premier mobile support, providing access to information while you are on the go		
vanced laptop support (incl. ClearType support, DualView, pow nagement improvements) - so you get as much work done while the road as while you are in the office.	●	●
Wireless connections - automatic 802.1x wireless network conf	●	●
Remote Desktop – remotely access your Windows XP Professi from another Windows PC, so you can work with all of your da applications while away from your office.	○	●
Offline Files and Folders - access to files & folders on a networ when disconnected from the server.	○	●
Highly responsive with the power to work on multiple tasks at once		
Fast start-up & power management improvements - faster boot resume times.	●	●
Multitasking - allow multiple applications to run simultaneousl	●	●
Scalable processor support – up to two-way multi-processor su	○	●
Keeps your data secure and maintains your privacy		
Internet Connection Firewall - automatically shields your PC fr unauthorized access when you are on the Internet.	●	●
Internet Explorer 6 privacy support - maintain control over you information when visiting Web sites.	●	●
Encrypting File System - protects sensitive data in files that are disk using the NTFS file system.	○	●
Access Control – restrict access to selected files, applications, ε resources.	○	●
Designed to work with Microsoft Windows Servers and management solutions		
Centralized administration - join Windows XP Professional sys Windows Server domain to take advantage of the full range of management and security tools.	○	●
Group Policy - simplifies the administration of groups of users computers.	○	●
Software Installation and Maintenance – automatically install, ε repair, or remove software applications.	○	●
Roaming User Profiles - access to all your documents and settir matter where you log on.	○	●
Remote Installation Service (RIS) – support for remote operatir installations where desktops can be installed across the network	○	●

243

Communicate efficiently with others around the world		
Single Worldwide Binary - enter text in any language and run a language version of Win32 applications on any language version Windows XP.	●	●
Multi-lingual User Interface (MUI) add-on - change the user in language to get localized dialog boxes, menus, help files, dictio and proofing tools etc.	○	

Note: " The above was taken for Microsoft web page
http://www.microsoft.com/windowsxp/home/evaluation/whyupgra
de/featurecomp.asp"

Windows XP Section – Introduction

Soon Windows XP will have a home on your computer and
everyone else's. Based on the Windows NT kernel, known for its
stability and performance, Windows XP brings a completely new
life to the home computer. Businesses have known of this for quite
some time with Windows NT 4.0 and Windows 2000. Now it is
your turn. Blue Screens of Death, Illegal Operations (at least in
that terminology), and interesting enough casual copying will be
outdated. Microsoft has spent their time and money to make
Windows XP not just an operating system, However, everything
you need in using a PC. They have tried many attempts to do this
However, XP is definitely a breakthrough. They have done this on
many; many fronts however, for the consumer there are a few that
are most notable.

Help, Support, and Recovery is one of the most important.
Microsoft has continued their PC Health initiative they used in
Windows Millennium However, on a completely new scale.
Windows XP Help and Support not only helps you with what is in
the program itself However, provides links to Windows Support
sites and will even search it for you and bring you back Support
Articles that may apply. Friends can help you in a completely new
way with Remote Assistance. Then as a last resort, System Restore
provides the answer.

Music and Entertainment is fully developed in Windows XP.
Windows Media Player 8 is actually usable on a daily basis now.
WMP8 has added new encoding technologies that surpass all of the
competition in video and in music form. WMP 64 bit rate is CD
quality and is half the size of a mp3.

Windows XP adds a lot more features than just here, however, this
is just the introduction.

How to create a boot disk

This is quite simple.

1: Go into MY COMPUTER

2: Have a floppy disk in your drive and then RIGHT click on on
the floppy drive and then click on FORMAT

3: You will be greeted with a number of options. The one you need
to select is "Create an MS-DOS start up disk".

4: Click ok

Note: This requires up to 5 floppy disks and DOES NOT contain ANY CD-ROM drivers to boot from. A proper CD-ROM boot up disk is going to be release by Microsoft after the Windows XP public release. You can however use you old Windows Me start-up disk if you would prefer, as long as you have not upgraded to an NTFS drive.

25 Things You Did not Know About XP

You can rename several files at one time within Explorer. A long overdue feature, in my opinion.

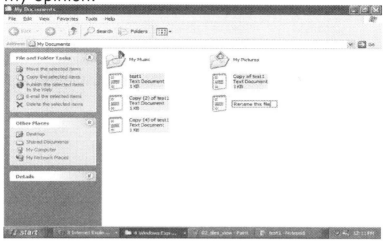

1. The tiles view is there for getting quick picture dimensions -- a wonderful thing for those of us who work with the Web. When you select an image, its dimensions will also be displayed in the Status bar (if it is turned on).

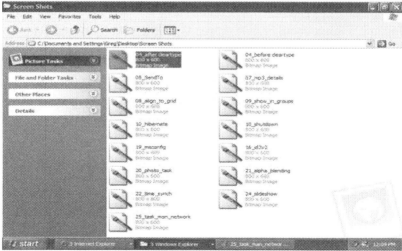

2. Check out the Details view if you have a ton of similar files in the folder. In one glance, you can view the number of pages, bit rate, details, and so

on. Of course, it depends on what it is you are trying to view.).

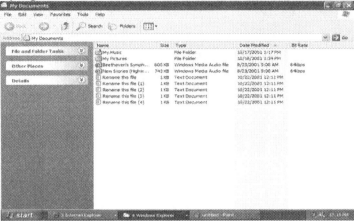

3. ClearType is a great reason to upgrade to XP. While it does have a noticeable impact on 2D performance, the view is spectacular. It is not just for LCD screens, contrary to popular belief. Font smoothing is so 20th century.

4. Your removable drives are automatically added to the SendTo menu. I cannot figure out how to get them out of there, as I never really use my floppy or Zip drives.

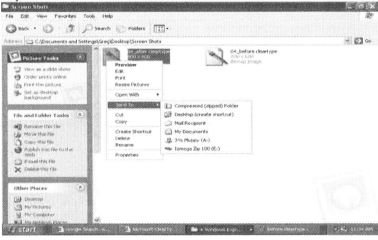

5. EXIF support is built into the Explorer shell. This allows you to see embedded information from untouched digital photos. This is another awesome feature for shutterbugs.

6. Details view in MP3 folders is necessary. It is very much like WiMP in the sense that you can view all sorts of song details from within the Explorer window.

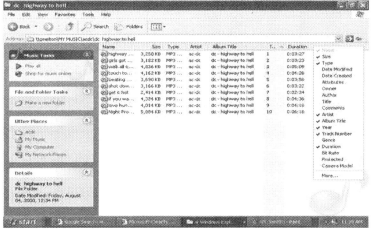

7. Being a neat freak, I appreciated the new Align to Grid feature for the Windows desktop. Now I do not have to right-click and Arrange every time I move a stupid icon. Try as you might, you cannot drag desktop icons off the screen with this option turned on.

8. Man, you have to play with the Show in Groups Arrange option. It is neat, and depending on how you have the folder set up, it will provide different sorting options (alphabetically by file type, general

file type, and so on). Very, very cool.

9. When you see the shutdown dialog pop up, hold onto the Shift key if you want to flip energy saving modes

10. WiMP will now grab cover shots and detailed information for your DVDs.

11. When you put in a CD with MP3s on it, XP asks you what you want to do with it. It does the same basic thing when you insert a picture CD or plug in a digital camera. Very friendly.

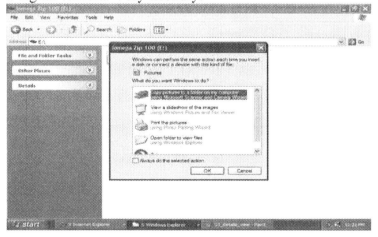

12. Icons in the System Tray are now displayed in high color. It is about time! Oddly enough, when you configure the System Tray (by right clicking on the Taskbar and selecting Properties), in the Notification area, someone forgot to update the old icons for Paint, Network, Calculator, and so on.

13. Zip file support is finally built into the OS. Yes, I know Me had it, too, However, I hate that OS.

14. No PowerToys ship with the Windows XP CD, although they will be available from Microsoft's site after October 25. They are a must for any user, experienced or not. Super Fast User Switcher, PowerToy Calculator, Alt-Tab replacement, Virtual Desktop Manager, Photo Toys, TweakUI, Command Window Here, Slideshow generator, Magnifier, HTML Generator, and TimerShot.

15. ID3v2 is supported throughout the OS (in WiMP 8.0 as well as in the Explorer shell). To edit an MP3's information, pull up its properties and flip to the Summary tab.

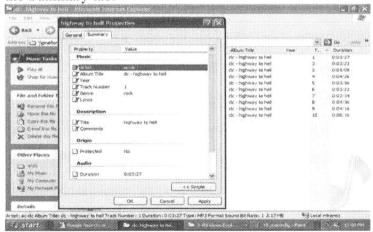

16. You can store/save your current Theme to the My Documents folder. On the surface, this feature appears to be back words compatible with classic Desktop Themes.

17. I think I have rebooted this computer less than 10 times, yet XP's boot process (from BIOS to desktop) is faster than it is ever been. Let me time the sucker. Hold on -- this should only take a minute. I take that back! It took me 45 seconds to get back up and running again.

18. Msconfig is back, baby. Windows 2000 users will appreciate its return. Of course, X-Setup works just fine on XP, too.

19. In folders designated for pictures, the Tasks pane will give you an option to print them. Choose your images, layout, printer, and so on. If you have a photo printer, this is a spectacular feature. If you choose not to work with the Tasks pane, you can simply open an image in the Windows Viewer and print from there to get to the same wizard.

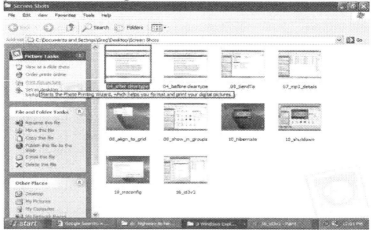

20. You would be surprised at how much alpha blending of icons improves the experience. No matter what wallpaper or background color you are

using, they will always look smooth.

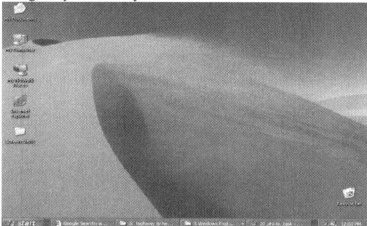

21. SNTP/NTP time synchronization is now built into the Date and Time applet. With it, you can connect to any Internet time-server. Never miss a meeting again!

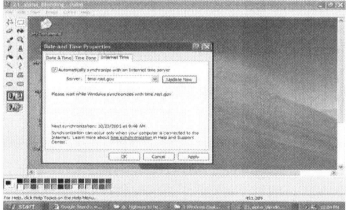

22. When Explorer crashes, the icons are restored in the System Tray. Finally, I verified this the other day when I ran into that weird gray screen problem.

23. XP comes with a basic slideshow screen saver --
perfect for showing off your recent vacation photos.

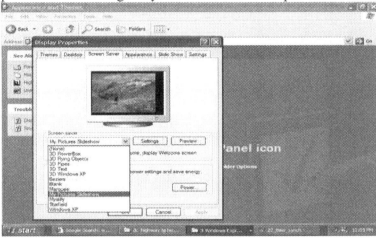

24. The Task Manager now has Networking
performance indicators. Right-click on the Taskbar
and select Task Manager for more.

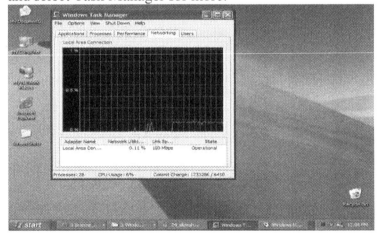

25 More Things You Did not Know About XP

1. You can now turn off thumbnail caching to save
disk space (via Folder Options). With TweakUI,

254

you can change the default dimensions of the thumbnail images.

2. Internet Explorer now has built-in support for Google (as long as you are using the search assistant).

3. They finally updated the card backs in Solitaire. Considering how many people play it on a regular basis, it is a notable improvement.

4. Go directly to the Start Menu properties by right clicking on the Start Button. Switch to the "classic" Start Menu if the new one annoys you. The "Highlight newly installed programs" feature is nice for download maniacs.

5. XP's moviemaker truly sucks; you cannot do ANYTHING with it. No transitions beyond a simple fade, no export options other than Windows Media, and so on.

   Just do not think you are going to film a businessman flying around your neighborhood and wind up producing an awesome -winning film using Windows XP. It is not going to happen with this crapplet.

6. Microsoft's marketing campaign is a bit misleading; you cannot play DVD movies without purchasing a third-party decoder first. While MP3s can be played out of the box, ripping music into this audio format is possible only through (again) third-party software.

7. Even with XP's built-in Internet Connection Firewall features, I still recommend Tiny Personal Firewall (freeware).

8. Most of you have here reports about the automatic grouping of open applications in the Taskbar (when you have several instances running, Windows will put them under the same Taskbar Button). Here is

something else I discovered: open Internet Explorer, then Notepad, then Internet Explorer again. Look at that. It puts the same apps next to each other, no matter the order in which they were opened.

9. Someone at Microsoft forgot to update the individual Administrative Tools and Offline webpage's folder icons. They are still ugly. Under the "Customize" tab of the folder properties dialog, you can assign a different icon for each and every folder.

10. The Windows help system has a wealth of new features. In one swoop, you can perform queries against the local database as well as the Microsoft Knowledge Base. However, I do not think the MSKB integration is working yet. For one, it does not return any results on basic terms. And it defaults to searching for Windows 2000 specific issues. Anyway, click the last icon in the toolbar (the document with a red checkmark in it). Tweak away!

11. The OS only comes with three Visual Styles -- which are lame to begin with. The Plus! site may have more available in time, However, who really knows?

12. I thought it was rather shortsighted that XP does not allow you to associate WMA sounds to your events. I mean, they are shoving the format down your throat in every other application. Why not here, too? Anyway, system (default) sounds have received a much-needed upgrade

13. In Windows 2000, you really could not make a boot disk. Sure, you could create a set of setup disks, However, nothing like a simple boot floppy. Right-click on the Floppy drive icon, select format, then place a checkmark in the "Create an MS-DOS startup disk". The MSDOS.SYS file contains W98EBD -- which leads me to believe that the files

were taken from Windows 98. This will not do you much good if you have an NTFS drive.

14. When was the last time you forgot your password? Uh, do not forget it for Windows XP until you create a password recovery disk. Under Related Tasks in the User Accounts Control Panel applet, click Prevent a forgotten password.

15. The Kodak Imaging Application that came with other versions of Windows has been replaced by the Windows Picture and Fax Viewer. It has a few built-in options; However, you cannot easily view the image at its full size. While this replacement is good enough, I miss the Kodak app already.

16. People think XP does not support plug-ins. That is not true -- it stopped supporting Netscape-style plug-ins.

17. Yes, you can hide inactive System Tray icons, However, why on Earth did not they line up the double-arrow indicators with those in the main Taskbar area? Another oversight by the design team, I am certain.

18. Window transparency works much better in XP than it ever did in 2000. Again, this speed difference could be attriHowever, ed to the video driver being used.

19. Passport is all over the place in Windows XP. However, you do not have to sign up for a new email account if you do not want to. Just use your current email address, and make a Passport password for it. Since I am not sure what Microsoft plans on doing with Passport, I just used my secret Hotmail account. You can change this any time via the User Accounts applet in the Control Panel.

20. Managing file associations is a dream. Right-click on a file, locate the updated Open With cascading menu (which now uses a program's default icon),

then click Choose Program if you want to change how the file is opened. In addition, if you do not know what program to associate a file with, there is a nice hyperlink included in the dialog to take you to a helpful Microsoft webpage.

21. The desktop properties dialog is extensive, However, scattered. For instance, the Themes tab is the first one you see, yet you have to flip to the Appearance tab in order to change how your interface works.

22. The volume mixer looks weird. However, the Main play control is not the same width as the other controls. Not to mention, they did not replace the yellow speaker icons for the other controls. And as if that was not enough, you can no longer tap ESC to quickly close the window.

23. Are you the type of person who notices speed increases (and decreases)? Well, as far as file operations are concerned, this is the snappiest version of Windows I have ever used. In Windows 2000, I would select a few files on the desktop, delete them, and then two seconds later, their icons would disappear. When I do the same thing in XP, the removal is immediate. Likewise, it takes far less time for me to open the Recycle Bin when it is filled with items now.

24. The default search "doggie" is annoying for power users; thank goodness, the new TweakUI will allow you to easily switch back to the "classic" Windows 2000 search feature. I do not know if this is a bug I uncovered; when I browse for a folder when I'm doing a Search, it shows me two My Documents folders. They each have the same folder structure inside of them

Enabling and Disabling the Windows XP Firewall

Windows XP contains its own firewall. A firewall is a security system that acts as a protective boundary between a network and the outside world. Internet Connection Firewall (ICF) is firewall software that is used to set restrictions on what information is communicated from your home or small office network to and from the Internet to your network.

If your network uses Internet Connection Sharing (ICS) to provide Internet access to multiple computers, ICF should be enabled on the shared Internet connection. However, ICS and ICF can be enabled separately. You should enable ICF on the Internet connection of any computer that is connected directly to the Internet. To check to see if ICF is enabled or to enable the firewall, see Enable or disable Internet Connection Firewall.

ICF also protects a single computer connected to the Internet. If you have, a single computer connected to the Internet with a cable modem, a DSL modem, or a dial-up modem, ICF protects your Internet connection. You should not enable ICF on VPN connections because it will interfere with the operation of file sharing and other VPN functions.

1 Enable the ICF by right clicking on your Internet or Network connection and then going to the ADVANCED option and ticking the ICF enable box.

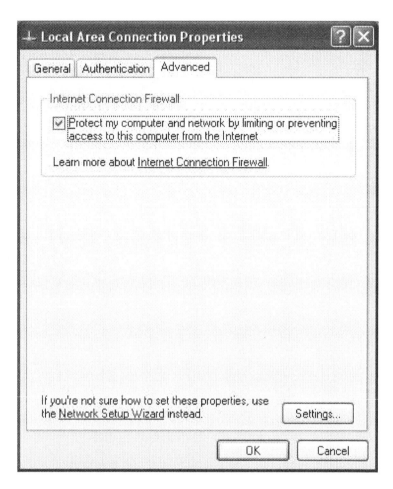

Adding Programs To Stay On The Start Menu

Right click on any .exe file in Explorer, My Computer, Desktop and select 'Pin to Start Menu', the program is then displayed on the start menu, above the separator line. To remove it, click the file on the start menu and select 'Unpin from Start Menu'. Below you can check the before and after shots.

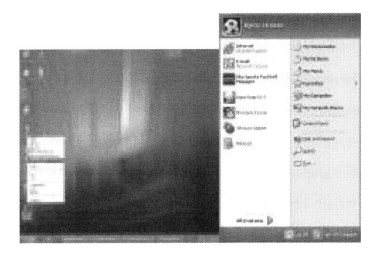

Make Use Of Your Windows Key

The Windows logo key, located in the bottom row of most computer Keyboards is a little-used treasure. Do not ignore it. It is the shortcut anchor for the following commands:

Windows: Display the Start menu
Windows + D: Minimize or restore all windows
Windows + E: Display Windows Explorer
Windows + F: Display Search for files
Windows + Ctrl + F: Display Search for computer
Windows + F1: Display Help and Support Center
Windows + R: Display Run dialog box
Windows + break: Display System Properties dialog box
Windows + shift + M: Undo minimize all windows
Windows + L: Lock the workstation
Windows + U: Open Utility Manager
Windows + Q: Quick switching of users (PowerToys only)
Windows + Q: Hold Windows Key, then tap Q to scroll thru the different users on your PC

Installing Netmeeting

Wondering how to install Netmeeting on Windows XP? Well you do not have to install it! Why? It is already pre-installed with Windows XP, However, (by design they say) it is not linked to anywhere on your programs menu. Here is how to load it:

1. Click START then RUN

2. Enter "conf" without the quotes

That is it - now you can Netmeet to your hearts content

Disable Error Reporting

As many of you would have noticed - every time a Microsoft program crashes in Windows XP - and Error Report comes up allowing you to send some information on the crash to Microsoft. Well this can get quite annoying, so here is how you disable it.

1. Open Control Panel
2. Click on Performance and Maintenance.
3. Click on System.
4. Then click on the Advanced tab
5. Click on the error-reporting Button on the bottom of the windows.
6. Select Disable error reporting.
7. Click OK
8. Click OK

Turn Off Thumbnail Caching

Another very basic tip here. Every time you go into a folder which contains either pictures or movies, Windows creates a thumbnail image so you can get an idea of what the picture/movie content will be. The thumbnail cache helps speed up access to the thumbnails instead of having them load up every time you go into a folder, However, each picture you have in a folder will take up around 2kb's, so imagine a folder with 200 photos and what size the cache could end up being.

The fact is though that these days having a thumbnail cache is not that important, the thumbnails load up here in my machine in seconds without it. Therefore, here is how you remove the caching system for thumbnails:

1. Click on "CONTROL PANEL" from the Start Menu.
2. Click on "FOLDER OPTIONS" in the Control Panel.
3. Click the view tab
4. Finally - tick the "DO NOT CACHE THUMBNAILS" box and then click APPLY.

Your Windows XP system will now no longer cache thumbnails. If you wish to go back to caching them, get back to the folder options menu as if we did about and unpick the box.

Change Internet Explorer Browser Title Text

Want to know how to customize the Title bar text of the Internet Explorer.

1. Click Start > Run > Type gpedit.msc
2. Click User Configuration > Windows Setting > Internet Explorer Maintenance > Browser User Interface
3. Double click on Browser Title
4. Click on Customize Title Bars
5. Change the text to what whatever you want
6. Click on Ok

Now you changed the title of your browser and you sure see what you wrote when you
open a New Widow.

Reading and **Understanding The Events Log**

For those of you that do not know. The event viewer in Windows XP maintains logs about program, security, and system events on your computer. You can use Event Viewer to view and manage the event logs, gather information about hard ware and software problems, and monitor Windows security events.

• To open Event Viewer, click Start, click Control Panel, double-click Administrative Tools, and then double-click Event Viewer.
• For information about using Event Viewer, in Event Viewer, on the Action menu, click Help.

Reading and **Understanding The Events Log**

For those of you that do not know. The event viewer in Windows XP maintains logs about program, security, and system events on your computer. You can use Event Viewer to view and manage the event logs, gather information about hard ware and software problems, and monitor Windows security events.

• To open Event Viewer, click Start, click Control Panel, double-click Administrative Tools, and then double-click Event Viewer.
• For information about using Event Viewer, in Event Viewer, on the Action menu, click Help.

Where has Scan Disk gone?

Scandisk is not a part of Windows XP - instead you get the improved CHKDSK. You can use the Error-checking tool to check for file system errors and bad sectors on your hard disk.

1. Open My Computer, and then select the local disk you want to check.

2. On the File menu, click Properties.

 3. On the Tools tab, under Error-checking, click Check Now.

4. Under Check disk options, select the Scan for and attempt recovery of bad sectors check box.

•   All files must be closed for this process to run. If the volume is currently in use, a message box will appear prompting you to indicate whether you want to reschedule the disk checking for the next time you restart your system. Then, the next time you restart your system, disk checking will run. Your volume will not be available to perform other tasks while this process is running.
•   If your volume is formatted as NTFS, Windows automatically logs all file transactions, replaces bad clusters, and stores copies of key information for all files on the NTFS volume.

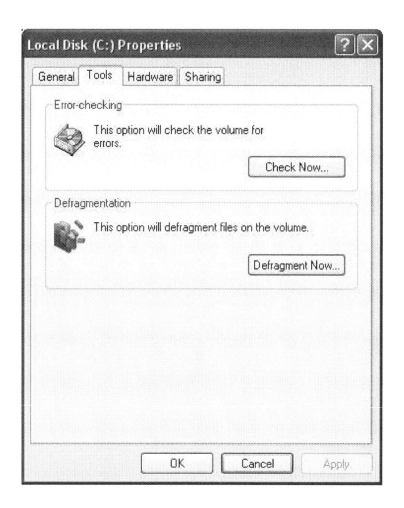

Speed Up Browsing

When you connect to a web site, your computer sends information back and forth. Some of this information deals with resolving the site name to an IP address, the stuff that TCP/IP really deals with, not words. This is DNS information and is used so that you will not need to ask for the site location each and every time you visit the site. Although Windows XP and Windows XP have a efficient DNS cache, you can increase its overall

performance by increasing its size.

You can do this with the registry entries below:

Windows Registry Editor Version 5.00

[HKEY_LOCAL_MACHINE\SYSTEM\CurrentControlSet\Servic
es\Dnscache\Parameters]
"CacheHashTableBucketSize"=dword:00000001
"CacheHashTableSize"=dword:00000180
"MaxCacheEntryTtlLimit"=dword:0000fa00
"MaxSOACacheEntryTtlLimit"=dword:0000012d

Make a new text file and rename it to dnscache.reg. Then copy and paste the above into it and save it. Merge it into the registry.

Never Re-Activate After Installation

If you have to reinstall Windows XP, you normally will have to reactivate too. Well not anymore. Just copy wpa.dbl after you activated the first time. It is located in the WINDOWS\system32 folder. Now if you reinstall Windows XP just copy the file back and you are up and running again.

Show Hidden Files & Folders

Wondering how to find files or folders that you have used before However, they seem to have vanished in Windows XP?

1. In any folder, that contains files. Click on the tools menu and select folder options.
2. Then click on the view tab.

3. Locate where it lists Hidden files and folders and select Show hidden files and folders.
4. Click OK.

Disable Boot up Splash Screen

You can, if you feel like it, disable the Windows XP boot up splash screen. Although this does not speed boot times at all, it does allow you to see if there are any boot up messages appearing on your computer that might otherwise be covered up.

1. Edit boot.ini
2. Add "/noguiboot" right after "/fastdetect".

You will need to restart your PC for the splash screen to disappear. To enable the splash screen again, just remove the switch that you added.

Removing The "Go" Button In Internet Explorer

There are a couple of ways in which you can remove the "Go" Button from Internet Explorer. The one we will go with is the easiest method.

Just right-click on the "Go" Button itself and uncheck it from the pull down list.

Using Active Movie

Ever wondered what happened to the good old Active Movie from Windows 9x? Well it is still around if you want to use it in Windows XP. Just create a shortcut with all of the following:

"%windir%\system32\rundll32.exe amovie.ocx,RunDll"

Make sure you omit the quotes and include the space. Enjoy!

Disabling Blue Screen Of Death Auto-Reboot

When you are running Windows XP, you may have noticed that every so often (rarely) that Windows reboots without you asking it to. This tends to be caused by a Blue Screen error. If you want to see what this error is, you will have to check the error log list because Windows reboots too quickly for you to read what happened. Well with this tip you can disable the Auto-Reboot so you can finally read, and see the blue screen error.

- Go to Start -> Control Panel -> System
- Go to Advanced
- Under the Startup and Recovery section, click Settings...
- Under System Failure un-check "Automatically restart"

Slow Shutdown?

Some people have noticed that they are experiencing a slow shutdown after installing Windows XP Home or Professional. Although this can be caused a number of ways, the most clear-cut one so far is happening on systems with an NVidia card installed with the latest set of drivers. A service called NVIDIA Driver Helper Service is loading up on start up and for whatever reason does not shut itself down properly. The service is not needed and can also increase the amount of memory available to your system. Here is how to disable it.

1. Go into your Control Panel

2. Select Administrative Tools and then click on Services

3. Right click on the file "NVIDIA Driver Helper Service" and then select STOP.

To stop this loading up every time you boot up your PC Right click it again and select properties - then where the option "Start-up

Type" is shown - make sure it is set at Manual like we have shown in the image below.

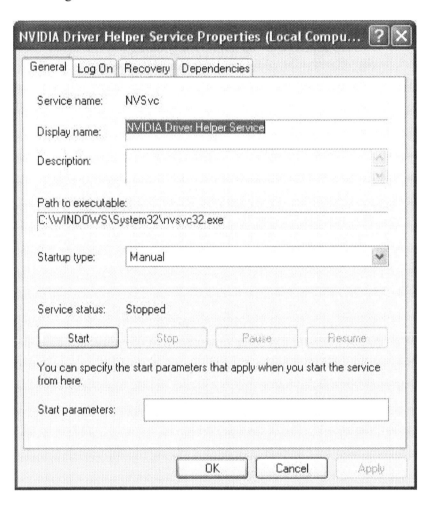

My Computer Will not Shut Down Itself After Installing XP

There are a number of users who are noticing that their PC will no longer automatically power down/shut off without pressing the power off Button on the computers unlike in Windows

Me/95/2000. There could be a number of reasons for this - However, the main one seems to be that ACPI is not enabled on the computer or in Windows XP. Here is how to try that out:

1. Click - Start - Control Panel - Performance and Maintenance - Power Options
Tab

2. Then click APM - Enable Advanced Power Management Support

Disabling The Windows XP Boot Logo

Incase you did not already know, It is possible to disable the Windows XP boot-up splash screen, although this only speeds up the boot process very slightly so there is not a real need to use this tweak.

1. Edit boot.ini
2. Add "/noguiboot" right after "/fastdetect".

Once you reboot, the splash screen will be gone. It can be re-enabled by removing the new switch.

Shutdown Windows XP Faster

When you shut down Windows XP, the OS tries its best to make sure that all services (they help run things like graphics, printers etc) are shut down. However, there are times when they do not close, thus Windows XP tries to give it the chance to shut down itself. This amount of time that windows waits for the service to close is stored in the system registry. If you modify this setting, then windows will shut down the service earlier. To modify the setting, follow the directions below:

- Start Regedit.

- Navigate to HKEY_LOCAL_MACHINE/SYSTEM/CurrentControlSet/Control.
- Click on the "Control" Folder.
- Select "WaitToKillServiceTimeout"
- Right click on it and select Modify.
- Set it to a value lower than 2000, say 1000 as a test.

Change The Taskbar Group Size

By default taskbar grouping will happen when you have three or more of the same program windows open. We have found the registry key to change the settings so that, if you prefer, Windows XP will wait till you open even more of the same program windows before they start to group. Here is an overview of Taskbar Grouping first:

Overview

The taskbar can become crowded with Button s when you are working with multiple programs at the same time. For this reason, Windows provides a feature to help you manage a large number of open documents and program items. The taskbar Button -grouping feature works in two ways. First, taskbar Button s for documents opened by the same program are always displayed in the same area of the taskbar so you can find your documents easily.

Second, if you have many documents open in the same program, Windows combines all the documents into one taskbar Button that is labeled with the name of the program. A triangle on the right side of the Button indicates that many documents are open in this program. The single Button provides access to all the open documents. To access one of the open documents, click the triangle on the taskbar Button, and then click a document name in the list. To act on all the open documents at the same time, use the right-click menu. For example, right clicking the triangle gives you a menu that lets you close all the open documents.

Sort Favorites/Programs Folders

This is as basic as our basic tips can get. If you would like to sort either your Favorites or Program menus into alphabetical order, all you have to do is right click in the menu and then click on "Sort By Name"

Changing The Internet Time Update Synchronisation

To change the interval that Windows updates the time using the internet timeservers via regedit, navigate to:

1. HKEY_LOCAL_MACHINE\SYSTEM\ControlSet001\Services \W32Time\TimeProviders\NtpClient
2. Select "SpecialPollInterval"
3. Change decimal value from 604800 to a different value in seconds. i.e.: 172800 (2 Days) or 86400 (1 Day) and so on.

I do not recommend changing this unless you are on a broadband connection.

On Screen Keyboard

Want to use an on screen Keyboard? Well it is this simple - Click on the start Button and select run. Then type in ok in the box and click OK.

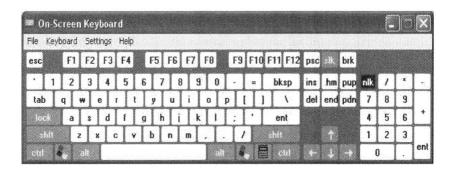

How to Prevent Windows Messenger from Running on Windows XP

Some of you dislike the fact Windows Messenger starts each time you start your computer. To prevent Windows Messenger 4.5 (or later) from running, use the following method: Start Registry Editor (Regedit.exe).

1. Locate and click the following registry key:

HKEY_LOCAL_MACHINE\Software\Policies\Microsoft

2. On the Edit menu, point to New, click Key, and then type Messenger for the name of the new registry key.
3. Locate and click the following registry key:

HKEY_LOCAL_MACHINE\Software\Policies\Microsoft\Messen ger

4. On the On the Edit menu, point to New, click Key, and then type Client for the name of the new registry key.
5. Locate and click the following registry key:

HKEY_LOCAL_MACHINE\Software\Policies\Microsoft\Messen ger\Client

6. On the Edit menu, point to New, click DWORD Value, and then type Prevent Run for the name of the new DWORD value.
7. Right-click the PreventRun value that you created, click Modify , type 1 in the Value data box, and then click OK .
8. Quit Windows Messenger.

Note: This tip is extracted from article Q302089 of the Microsoft Windows XP Knowledge Base.

Boot Defragment

A very important new feature in Microsoft Windows XP is the ability to do a boot defragment. This basically means that all boot files are placed next to each other on the disk drive to allow for faster booting. By default this option is enabled however, some upgrade users have reported that it is not on their setup.

1. Start Regedit.
2. Navigate to HKEY_LOCAL_MACHINE\SOFTWARE\Microsoft\Dfrg\BootOptimizeFunction
3. Select Enable from the list on the right.
4. Right on it and select Modify.
5. Change the value to Y to enable and N to disable.
6. Reboot your computer.

How to cheat at Minesweeper

Who has ever won to Minesweeper? If you are tired of losing all the time you can try this nice cheat that will basically reveals mines:

1. Start Minesweeper,
2. Type "xyzzy" without the quotes,
3. Hit Shift and Enter at the same time,
4. Minimize all application windows that hide the desktop. The uppermost pixel in the top left corner of your desktop will turn black when you mouse over a mine and white when it is safe to click.

This tip also works with Windows 2000 & Windows NT 4.0.

ADVANCED

How Do I Edit The Registry? To run regedit just click on the start Button and then select run. Then type "regedit" (Without the quotes) in to the box and click ok. Once this is done - you are in

RegEdit - the program that can be used to edit the Registry in Windows XP.

Clear Out Pagefile On Shutdown

When working on your PC, having Word documents or webpage's open means that the pages get loaded into the RAM, to save RAM Windows tends to put various files into your Page File (Like a cache system). Microsoft has left an option to clear out the Pagefile on shutdown off as default; here is the way to switch it on. Take note, this increases shutdown time.

1. Start Regedit.
2. Navigate to HKEY_LOCAL_MACHINE\SYSTEM\CurrentControlSet\Control \Session Manager\Memory Management
3. Select Clear Page File At Shutdown from the list on the right.
4. Right on it and select Modify.
5. Change the value to 1 to enable.
6. Reboot your computer.

Disabling unnecessary services

Services are programs that start up when your computer boots. They continue to run in the background while your PC is on, some services load automatically, some when a program is used. Some of these services are not needed by various users and can be safely disabled. However, BE WARNED there are some of the services that MUST not be disabled. To get a good idea what can and cannot be removed check out http://www.blkviper.com/WinXP/servicecfg.htm for a very detailed list. Remember, you can always turn the service back on if you find out that you need it in the future. Below is the procedure to turn off a service.

- Click the start Button .

- Click on Control Panel.
- Click on Administrative Tools.
- Click Services.
- Once the services window has loaded, you are now able to turn off any unneeded services.
- For instructional purposes we are going to turn off the Printer Spooler (Which is not needed if you do not have a printer installed) service.
- Find this service in the list and select it with the mouse.
- Right click and select Properties.
- Once the properties windows has loaded find the Start up type drop down box and select disable.
- Then finally, click ok and the next time the computer starts the service will no longer be loaded.

Turning Off System Beeps

Although we do not recommend this tip very much as having the warning beep etc can help you find out when problems happen, it does annoy some people - We have a simple registry editing way of turning them off.

- Load Regedit.
- Navigate to HKEY_CURRENT_USER\Control Panel\Sound
- On the left hand side of the screen, find Beep on the list.
- Right click on it and select Modify
- Change the value equal to no
- Reboot your computer
- The beeps will then vanish - if you wish them to return change the equal value back to yes.

How to Display a Details Tab in Each Device Properties Dialog Box

Windows XP can display in each device properties dialog box a supplementary tab named 'details' that lists advanced information about the current device that is mainly dedicated to administrators or developers. To permanently display the 'details' tab in each device properties dialog box of the device manager, use the following method:

1. Click Start/Control Panel,
2. Double click 'System',
3. Click the Advanced tab,
4. Click 'Environment Variables',
5. Locate the 'System variables' frame,
6. Click New,
7. In the Name label, type: "DEVMGR_SHOW_DETAILS"
8. In the Value label type 1 and then click OK, OK and OK,
9. Now in open the device manager, double click a device of your choice and look: you have a new details tab with tons of information's to dig in.

Turning off System Restore

When you install Windows XP (Or when it comes pre-installed), Windows XP keeps a backup of system files in the System Volume Information folder. This system can take up large amounts of space on your Hard Drive, which you may not want it to. If you no longer want Windows to back up your system files please do the following:

1. Open the Control Panel
2. Double click on system
3. Click the System Restore tab
4. Check "Turn off System Restore on all drives
5. Click Apply
6. You can now delete the System Volume Information folder.

Warning! If you turn this off you will not be able to use Windows System Restore to restore your system in case of failure.

Turning Off Indexing Speeds Up Windows XP

As some of you will already know, Windows XP keeps a record of all files on the hard disk to try and improve searching speed. The only downside to all of this is that your PC will have to be indexing all of the files, so if you do not use search very much you can disable this feature:

• Open my computer
• Right click on one of your hard drive icons and then select properties.
• At the bottom of the window you should see "Allow indexing service to index this disk for faster searches," uncheck this and click then click on ok.

A new window will pop up and select apply to all folders and subfolders. Once complete, it takes a few more minutes to make sure that indexing is now

Disable Bootup Splash Screen

You can, if you feel like it, disable the Windows XP boot up splash screen. Although this does not speed boot times at all, it does allow you to see if there are any boot up messages appearing on your computer that might otherwise be covered up.

1. Edit boot.ini
2. Add " /noguiboot" right after "/fastdetect".

You will need to restart your PC for the splash screen to disappear. To enable the splash screen again, just remove the switch that you added.

Removing The "Go" Button In Internet Explorer

There are a couple of ways in which you can remove the "Go" Button from Internet Explorer. The one we will go with is the easiest method.

Just right-click on the "Go" Button itself and uncheck it from the pull down list.

Disabling Blue Screen Of Death Auto-Reboot

When you are running Windows XP, you may have noticed that every so often (rarely) that Windows reboots without you asking it to. This tends to be caused by a Blue Screen error. If you want to see what this error is, you will have to check the error log list because Windows reboots too quickly for you to read what happened. Well with this tip you can disable the Auto-Reboot so you can finally read, and see the blue screen error.

- Go to Start -> Control Panel -> System
- Go to Advanced
- Under the Startup and Recovery section, click Settings...
- Under System Failure un-check "Automatically restart

Show Hidden Files & Folders

Wondering how to find files or folders that you have used before However, they seem to have vanished in Windows XP?

1. In any folder, that contains files. Click on the tools menu and select folder options.
2. Then click on the view tab.

3. Locate where it lists Hidden files and folders and select Show hidden files and folders.
4. Click OK.

Adding Programs to Stay On The Start Menu

Right click on any .exe file in Explorer, My Computer, Desktop and select 'Pin to Start Menu', the program is then displayed on the start menu, above the separator line. To remove it, click the file on the start menu and select 'Unpin from Start Menu'

Disable Error Reporting

As many of you would have noticed - every time a Microsoft program crashes in Windows XP - and Error Report comes up allowing you to send some information on the crash to Microsoft. Well this can get quite annoying, so here is how you disable it.

1. Open Control Panel
2. Click on Performance and Maintenance.
3. Click on System.
4. Then click on the Advanced tab
5. Click on the error-reporting Button on the bottom of the windows.
6. Select Disable error reporting.
7. Click OK
8. Click OK

Reading and Understanding The Events Log

For those of you that do not know. The event viewer in Windows XP maintains logs about program, security, and system events on your computer. You can use Event Viewer to view and manage the event logs, gather information about hard ware and software problems, and monitor Windows security events.

- To open Event Viewer, click Start, click Control Panel, double-click Administrative Tools, and then double-click Event Viewer.
- For information about using Event Viewer, in Event Viewer, on the Action menu, click Help.

How to Prevent Windows Messenger from Running on Windows XP

Some of you dislike the fact Windows Messenger starts each time you start your computer. To prevent Windows Messenger 4.5 (or later) from running, use the following method:

1. Start Registry Editor (Regedit.exe).
2. Locate and click the following registry key: HKEY_LOCAL_MACHINE\Software\Policies\Microsoft
3. On the Edit menu, point to New, click Key, and then type Messenger for the name of the new registry key.
4. Locate and click the following registry key: HKEY_LOCAL_MACHINE\Software\Policies\Microsoft\Messenger
5. On the On the Edit menu, point to New, click Key, and then type Client for the name of the new registry key.
6. Locate and click the following registry key: HKEY_LOCAL_MACHINE\Software\Policies\Microsoft\Messenger\Client
7. On the Edit menu, point to New, click DWORD Value, and then type PreventRun for the name of the new DWORD value.

8. Right-click the PreventRun value that you created, click Modify , type 1 in the Value data box, and then click OK .
9. Quit Windows Messenger.

This tip is extracted from article Q302089 of the Microsoft Windows XP Knowledge Base.

Chapter 36

Home networking general

You have more than one computer in your home; you quickly discover what a hassle it is to be shoved aside when someone else needs the printer--which happens to be attached to your PC. You are also probably tired of running up and down the stairs to transfer files using floppy disks. And no one likes fighting over the only computer with Internet access. No wonder you are interested in home networking.

There was a time when this flexibility was a luxury reserved for the brave souls who threaded cables behind their walls to set up an ethernet network--and had mastered the arcane secrets of networking kung fu. However, over the past few years, a variety of home networking packages have appeared on the scene, and they are relatively easy to use. You can use your home's existing wiring--or in some cases, no wires at all.

I cover three different options here, based on the three established home networking stand port s: HomePNA 2.0 (Home Phone line Networking Alliance), which centers on your home's phone line system; HomePlug, which uses your existing power lines; and the 802.11b (Wi-Fi) stand port , which lets you go wireless. (There is also the more recent Wi-Fi5, also known as 802.11a, Wi-Fi's speedier successor.)

For shopping advice, product info, and details about how each technology works, read "How to Buy Home Networking Products." And if you are interested in finding out how the different technologies performed in PC World lab testing, go to "How Fast Are They Really?"

Be Prepared

Setting up a home network will go much more smoothly if you prepare a few things before and, no matter which option you choose. Although all networking kits come with adapters and the other components you need, such as phone line cables or USB cables, you will still want to have a few other things worked out before you plug anything in.

Visit the home networking company's Web site and make sure you have the most current drivers for your operating systems. You might have Windows Me on your PCs at home, for instance, and you may not get the right drivers for Me on the CD bundled with the networking kit.

Have your Windows installation CDs hand y for each PC to be networked; you may need to install Windows' own network drivers while setting up your home network.

Choose a name for your network (also referred to as a workgroup). Something descriptive is usually best, such as your family name or the name of your small business. Wireless networks will also need another name (a network identification code or SSID, which stand s for Service Set Identifier). It does not matter if the workgroup name and SSID are the same.

Decide on unique names for each computer. Although you can use literal, descriptive names like "Office" or "Games", you might as well be creative. I once named a dozen computers after famous comedians from the 1940s and 1950s.

How to Set Up Your Home Network Consider the ConfigurationTelephone Tag: HomePNA 2.0Power to the People: Home Plug The Wireless World: 802.11b (Wi-Fi)

Consider the Configuration

You will also want to plan how your network will be configured. At the bare minimum, a home network lets you print from any computer and access files from other computers without leaving your chair.

Remember: Most, However, not all, printers can be shared. To find out if your printer can be shared, open Control Panel and select Printers. Right-click your printer icon, and choose Properties. If there is a Shared tab in the dialog box that appears, click the tab and make sure the share option is selected. You are ready to share the printer.

You can also share an Internet connection, However, methods vary: Every version of Windows from Windows 98 on includes Microsoft's built-in Internet Connection Sharing, and some home network packages have their own software. The only problem with this setup is that the computer connected to the Internet (the server or host) has to be turned on to share its connection with the other computers (the clients). If this is inconvenient, there is a solution: You can use a gateway with a built-in router--a piece of hard ware that hand les Internet traffic a little like a switchbox port . This device is commonly referred to simply as a router.

You should also consider encryption. Any determined person can gain access to an unencrypted network without too much trouble.

With a HomePlug network, for example, someone could get access by tapping into the power line in a shared wall in an apartment building or hotel. Encryption scrambles data so that only your network understand s what its computers are saying to each other. The process involves creating your own encryption key--a series of letters and numbers, like a password--according to the encryption software instructions.

Wireless networks and HomePlug have encryption built into the stand port; HomePNA does not. For HomePNA, you will have to install another form of protection, such as a firewall program. With a wireless network, it is imperative that you set up encryption--remember, there is no physical barrier. Be aware, though, that the wireless security protocol is widely reported as inadequate--you should think about adding another layer of defense, like firewall software. Check out PC World's review of the latest personal firewall packages in "Protect Your PC".

Finally, there is the issue of dynamic versus static (or "fixed") IP addresses. An IP address is a numeric identifier--four sets of up to three digits separated by dots (such as 123.456.7.89) assigned to a device on a network. In many cases, the network you are connecting to issues your PC a temporary IP address when you log in, which you keep for the duration of your session. This is a dynamic IP address, and it suits most people just fine.

Nevertheless, if you are more ambitious and want to set up a Web site, or a printer or other device that can be accessed over the Internet, you will need a static IP address, one that never changes. Your Internet service provider has to give you a static IP address for the Net--and this usually costs extra. And many ISPs do not allow home users to run servers.

Telephone Tag: HomePNA 2.0

Companies such as Netgear, Linksys, and Proxim offer HomePNA packages.

What is good about HomePNA? It uses your household's existing telephone circuitry as its network wiring, and it is the easiest of the three-stand port s to install and use. HomePNA uses a distinct frequency on your phone line, so someone can talk on the phone or use a fax machine without interfering with your multiplayer game of Quake.

What is bad about HomePNA? Your computers all have to be near phone jacks. If you have more than one phone line, make sure all the jacks you plan to use are for the same phone number.

How to Set Up a HomePNA Network

HomePNA adapters come in three flavors: USB or PCI (for desktop computers), and PC Card (for notebooks). If you plan to share a high-speed Internet connection, you will also need an ethernet bridge ($180 and up)--like a gateway--on the system that uses the broadband modem, instead of an adapter. The ethernet bridge is hooked up to the PC that is connected to the broadband modem; no adapter is required for this PC.

Repeat the following steps for each computer:

Turn off the computer and install the manufacturer's adapter. If you are putting a PCI card into a desktop computer, you will have to open the case to do so.

Plug the adapter into a phone jack. If a telephone or fax machine is already using the jack, plug the phone or fax into the adapter first. If you are short on phone jacks, you may want to use a two-way splitter to share the jack.

Turn the computer on. Windows will detect the adapter and prompt you to install the driver from the included CD-ROM. Follow the on-screen instructions. Depending on the package you are using, you might also be prompted for the computer's name. (Remember what I said about being prepared?)

Restart the computer.

If you plan to share an Internet connection and do not have a router, install the Internet-sharing software (if included by the manufacturer) or use the Internet Connection Sharing software in Windows 98 Second Edition and Millennium Edition. Designate the computer that will connect directly to the Internet as the server; the others are clients. Remember to install firewall software on the server to protect all the PCs on your network.

Now you can invite your friends over for Quake III tournaments.

Companies including Linksys, GigaFast, and Asoka USA make HomePlug products.

What is good about HomePlug? Like HomePNA, HomePlug is easy to get rolling. Just plug one end of the adapter into a computer's USB port and the other end into a power outlet. And the odds are that you have got more power outlets than phone jacks.

What is bad about HomePlug? Being tethered to a power outlet can still be limiting; you also have to make sure you do not plug a HomePlug adapter into a surge suppressor or line conditioner-- your signal will likely be wiped out. And if you are using a notebook with a USB port, you will still have to carry around a big, bulky HomePlug adapter. There are no PC Card HomePlug adapters.

How to Set Up a HomePlug Network

With a HomePlug network, you simply attach one end of a brick-shaped adapter to your machine's USB or ethernet port, and use a cable to plug the other end into an electrical outlet.

If you plan to use HomePlug to share a high-speed Internet connection over power lines, you will need to use a HomePlug ethernet bridge ($180 and up) and a router. You can use just a bridge if your PCs already have ethernet adapters installed--you connect the adapters to the ethernet port of your cable or DSL modem. On the other hand, if your PC does not have an ethernet adapter However, does have a USB port, you can use a power-line USB adapter to share the PC's Internet connection. You also need Internet Connection Sharing software to share an Internet connection.

Install the bridge on the computer that connects to the Internet. To do this, you might have to install a second ethernet card. (If you already have a high-speed modem, which uses its own ethernet connection, you will need a second ethernet card to install the bridge.) Then, plug the bridge's RJ-45 cable into this second ethernet card. Then plug the bridge into an electrical outlet. If you have a router, connect the bridge to the ethernet port on the router.

Install the network configuration software from the CD that came with the HomePlug kit. You will be prompted for a network password.

Install the Internet Connection Sharing software, making sure to identify this PC as the server.

Then, on every other computer, install the HomePlug USB adapters. On the other hand, on PCs that have ethernet ports, you can use an ethernet bridge as an adapter. The benefit? The ethernet bridge tends to be slightly faster than a USB adapter.

Install the network configuration software. You will be prompted for a network password. Enter the same one you used for the bridge.

Install the adapter by plugging it into the computer's USB port. Windows will detect the adapter and prompt you to install the driver. You will find that on the CD-ROM in the HomePlug package.

Restart your PC. You are now ready to surf from the living room, or wherever you have a PC.

The Wireless World: 802.11b (Wi-Fi)

Netgear, Intel, D-Link, Proxim, and Linksys all offer both 802.11b (Wi-Fi) and 802.11a (Wi-Fi5) products.

What is good about wireless? Small, lightweight radio antennas give you the freedom to move around within their range. Hotels, airports, and even some coffee shops are setting up 802.11b access points for easy public wireless Internet access.

What is bad about wireless? Speeds drop off with distance, or if there are too many obstacles between two computers. There may also be interference problems between 802.11b antennas and other 2.4-GHz devices, such as cordless phones and microwaves. Note: At this point, you cannot use 802.11b and 802.11a products on the same network.

The basic form of wireless network is the ad hoc network; each computer communicates directly with the other, and the Internet connection is shared from one computer with a modem. An infrastructure network, on the other hand, uses an access point or wireless gateway (or router), so your adapters communicate with the access point, which works like a central transmitter/receiver.

An access point is a wireless hard ware device that allows a wireless network to connect to a wired network. Many access points come with a built-in gateway that connects to the Internet. Installing an access point is much like installing an adapter, except that you must also duplicate information from your modem's network configuration, such as your user name and password for your ISP. Check the manufacturer's documentation for specific instructions.

When it comes to adapters, you can find PCI and PC Card s for both 802.11b and 802.11a, plus USB 1.1 adapters for 802.11b. (You will not find any USB 1.1 adapters for 802.11a because they are too slow for the newer stand port.)

How to Set Up a Wireless Network

Follow this procedure on each computer:

Install the adapter according to the manufacturer's instructions. (If you are using a PCI adapter, you will have to turn off the computer, open the casing, insert the adapter into a free PCI slot, and restart the computer.)

Windows will detect the adapter and prompt you to install the driver on the included CD-ROM.

Install the network software that usually comes with the hard ware. You will be prompted for the computer's name, and asked if the current computer is meant to be the server or client for Internet access.

Restart the computer.

Now you have to create a profile--the collection of settings that let you use the network. You can have several different profiles, so that if you take your laptop to the office or the local networked coffee house, you have only to switch profiles to instantly connect to their network. To create a profile, run the configuration program that is part of the network software.

Set the mode to ad hoc (the mode may be set as peer-to-peer) if you are not using an access point, or infrastructure if you are.

Enter the network name. If you are using an ad hoc network, set the channel (a number from 1 to 11). All adapters on a network must use the same channel. (With an infrastructure network, the client automatically configures itself to the channel with the strongest signal.)

Enter your encryption key--a series of letters and numbers, like a password--according to the vendor's instructions.

What are you waiting for? Grab your notebook, head out, and check your e-mail.

Tips

The best thing you can do to make your home network a success is to plan.

What do you want to do with your network?

What do you want to connect? Make a list.

How do your computers, printers, and other components connect to each other?

Where are the components in your house? Draw a map.

What networking parts do you need? Make a list.

Wiring methods with Ethernet

Make an Ethernet network cable (includes Web video)

Most importantly, be flexible about your networking solutions.

Super secret tip: Many network interface cards and Wi-Fi adapters contain exactly the same chipsets. Keep this in mind when you are shopping around for parts and you are comparing prices.

Another super secret tip: Your network can be flexible and easy to grow, especially if you stick to popular components.

Internet Connection Sharing: Setting Up a Router

It only takes about 30 minutes to set up a router that will let you share your broadband connection with multiple computers.

How to setup a Router?

For most of us, there are only two choices for a broadband Internet connection: DSL or cable. Therefore, you make the phone call, schedule a time, and the technician comes to hook it up. Within an hour, you have a blazing fast Internet connection for one computer. However, what if you have a home network and other people want go online at the same time? Are they out of luck? Do they have to wait for your surfing frenzy to end?

No, they do not. All you have to do is follow the steps below, and you can share that rocket Internet connection with everyone on your network. Best of all, setting it up takes about 30 minutes.

Yesterday, we showed you how to run Proxy on your system to share your Internet access. Today, we will show you a hard ware router that does the same thing. A hard ware solution may be more expensive; However, when you use a hard ware router instead of Proxy software, you do not have to leave the main machine on.

How routers work

With a stand port broadband setup, you are assigned a single public IP address. When you use a router, it assumes that IP address. The router then assigns the computers on the network private IP addresses. All Internet traffic from your computers goes to the router and is funneled through the single public IP address.

The router's IP address is a factor when playing games online. Only one computer on your network will be able to connect to the same game at the same time. The game server only sees the one public IP address.

However, you can host a game so computers at home can connect behind the router, and others can connect from the Internet through the router. If you do need a public IP address for each computer, you will have to pay a nominal monthly fee to your ISP (approximately $5 per IP address per month).

Step 1: Round Up the Hard ware

Step 2: Hard ware Setup

Step 3: Software Setup

Step 4: Verify Your TCP/IP Setup

Step 5: Router Software Setup

Step 1: Round Up the Hard ware

Check your broadband modem before you start this project. If it connects to your machine via USB, see if you can get a modem with an Ethernet connection from your provider. If not, you will not be able to use an external hard ware router; you will have to dedicate a machine to that connection.

Routers

The routers we recommend are the Linksys and Netgear routers. Prices range between $100 and $150.

I just bought one from Linksys that does both Ethernet and 802.11b (wireless), the BEFW11S4 -- EtherFast Wireless AP + cable/DSL router with 4-port switch.

NICS

You need one NIC (network interface card) per computer. The NIC can be a PCI or ISA card   that goes inside your machine, or a USB or parallel port adapter.

If you have the cash, you can go wireless with an 802.11b network. It is awesome if you own a notebook.

Cables

One Ethernet cable (RJ-45) per computer with enough length to reach the router.

If you already have a network with a hub, you may need an RJ-45 Ethernet crossover cable.

Step 2: Hard ware Setup

Install the NICs in your computers, along with their appropriate drivers.

Choose a location for the router to reside. The cables from each computer will need to reach this location. do not forget that the cable from the modem will need to reach the router as well. That means you will probably put the router close to your broadband modem.

Using an Ethernet cable, connect each computer to the local ports on the router.

If you are using a hub, connect the uplink port on the hub to a local port on the router.

If your hub does not have an uplink port, use an Ethernet crossover cable to connect a normal hub port to a local port on the router.

Connect the Internet port, or WAN port, on your router to your cable or DSL modem with a stand port Ethernet cable (your modem will usually come with one).

Plug in your router and allow it to initialize. It will perform a self-test and verify its connection to the Internet. Typically, there is a set of lights on the front panel of the router that will show link status. Refer to the instruction manual for specifics.

Hard ware setup done. Now on to the software

Step 3: Software Setup

Set up the software on your computers to talk to the router. To install network software:

Right-click on Network Neighborhood and choose Properties.

If you do not have a TCP/IP protocol installed for your network card, click the Add Button.

Choose Protocol, and click the Add Button.

Click the Have Disk Button.

Enter the path where the drivers are located (A:, D:, and so on), and click OK.

Choose the TCP/IP protocol for your NIC, and click OK.

The network software will install; you may be prompted for your Windows CD or your NIC driver disk.

If you do not have a client installed for your computer, click the Add Button.

Choose Client and click the Add Button.

Choose Microsoft, choose Client for Microsoft Networks, and click the Add Button.

The network software will install; you may be prompted for your Windows CD or your NIC driver disk Under Primary Network Logon, click Drop Down Menu, and choose Client for Microsoft Networks.

In the list of network components installed, choose the TCP/IP protocol for your NIC, and click Properties.

Under the IP Address tab, choose Obtain an IP address automatically.

Click OK.

Click OK.

Your computer may reboot.

Step 4: Verify Your TCP/IP Setup

Step 5: Router Software Setup

Now you need to set up the software in the router. The following steps are for the Netgear Cable/DSL router RT311 (complete instructions are in the manual). These steps may be slightly different for each router. Refer to the instruction manual for help.

You can set up the router software using your web browser, or a telnet program. Using the web browser is easiest.

You will need your account information provided by your broadband supplier.

Start your Web browser.

In the address location, type: http://192.168.0.1

You will be prompted for a login and password. Your manual will give you the default settings.

Enter your host name provided by your ISP.

Enter your ISP's domain name

If your router prompts you for encapsulation, your setting will probably be the default: Ethernet, unless specified by your ISP.

When prompted for WAN IP address information, allow your router to receive and assign everything automatically.

If your ISP allows access from only one MAC address, you will need to choose the option of spoofing the MAC address and enter the corresponding local IP address.

Click Finish

Enter a URL and **see if it works.**

If you cannot reach the URL, reboot the router and wait for it to initialize. Then reboot your computer and try again.

If you still cannot reach the URL, unplug the cable modem for one minute, plug the modem back in, reboot the router, and wait for it to initialize. Then reboot your computer and try again.

Boot sequence

For stability, it is best to leave your router and cable modem on all the time. If you do need to turn it off, always turn components on in this order:

Cable Modem (wait for it to initialize)

Router (wait for it to initialize)

Computer

Your router acts as a DHCP server. It will assign IP addresses to your computers as they are booted up, so you need to make sure your network is working.

Once your machine boots:

Click the Start Button, and click Run.

In the blank, type "winipcfg.exe"

In the IP Configuration window, click the drop-down menu and choose your NIC

The following information should appear:

IP: should be between 192.168.0.2 and 192.168.0.31

Gateway: 192.168.0.1

Subnet: 255.255.255.0

If you do not get this information, reboot the router and wait for it to initialize. Then reboot your computer and try again.

www.ingramcontent.com/pod-product-compliance
Lightning Source LLC
Chambersburg PA
CBHW051224050326
40689CB00007B/800